INDEX

Preface

Evidentiary Realism aims to articulate a particular form of realism in art that portrays and reveals evidence from complex social systems.

The project *Evidentiary Realism* reflects on post-9/11 geopolitics, increasing economic inequalities, the erosion of civil rights, and environmental disasters. It builds on the renewed appreciation of the exposure of truth in the context of the cases of WikiLeaks, Edward Snowden, the Panama Papers, and the recent efforts to contend with the post-factual era.

Contemporary sharing and processing of information in an open global collaborative environment entails an amplified sense of reality. Leaks, discoveries, and facts are collectively verified and disseminated among numerous distribution networks. Techniques of presentation and engaging the public have been evolving in the same direction—through reconfiguration of media and languages, the evidence is presented in a variety of strategies and artifacts in dialogue with contemporary art practices.

Evidentiary Realism focuses on artworks that prioritize formal aspects of visual language and mediums; diverging from journalism and reportage, they strive to provoke visual pleasure and emotional responses. The evidence is presented through photography, film, drawing, painting, and sculpture, with strong references to art history. In particular, these artists also theoretically articulate the aesthetic, social, and documentary functions of their mediums in relation to the subject matter they investigate.

Some of the evidentiary realist works break down visibility to abstraction to underline the limits of seeing, while others use figuration or synthesis to enhance insight. The encoded information and nuanced details behind the works point to large, highly complex realities that come into focus through the factual evidence shown. Yet these enigmatic and seductive works serve as evidence of the opaque and intricate apparatus of our reality.

The process of translating investigations and documents into artworks underpins the idea of art as evidence. Such practices adopted by emerging and established artists of today can be traced to the works of Hans Haacke, Mark Lombardi, and Harun Farocki, who were some of the first artists invested in decoding complex systems of power and conveying them in bold artistic forms.

The creation of evidentiary artworks is the realism of today's world, which is trying to control, predict, and quantify itself. Evidentiary realists examine such complexity to condemn, document, and inform through compelling artworks, giving form to a particular documentary and investigative art practice.

Evidentiary Realism

Evidentiary Realism

by Paolo Cirio

Paolo Cirio writes on the impulse and tendency of forensic, documentary, and investigative aesthetics. He discusses the term *Evidentiary Realism*, the context from which it emerges, and the tension between the social and the subjective in modern art history, which now can be identified with the decline of post-structuralist aesthetics and the return of realism.

Naturally, in the struggle with falsehood we must write the truth, and this truth must not be a lofty and ambiguous generality [but] something practical, factual, undeniable, something to the point [..] taking away from these words their rotten, mystical implications.

Bertolt Brecht, *Writing the Truth, Five Difficulties*, 1935.

Realism is out of sight

The real is present and concrete, yet complexity, scale, speed, and opacity hide it from sight. The contemporary features of the social landscape are unintelligible at first glance. Although we see the shocking results of our social reality, we are nonetheless often unable to see the systems and processes that generate such conditions. Realism in art returns through intersecting documentary, forensic, and investigative practices that contemporary realist artists utilize to bring to light the unseeble beneath the formation of our society.

Realism traditionally portrays social oppression, visually illustrating people and situations truthfully and accurately. In the visual arts, it has primarily been expressed through figurative painting, photography, and film. Thus, realism today can be conceptualized as an expansion of ways of seeing and portraying contemporary social complexities, while maintaining the concern of presenting subject matter factually within the aesthetics of visual language. However, this particular realism looks beyond visible social conditions. *Evidentiary Realism* examines the underpinning economic, political, legal, linguistic, and cultural structures that impact society at large. These evolving social fields are highly interconnected and often too complex and high-speed to grasp—if not secret, imperceptible, opaque, or manipulated by advanced rhetorical devices. Reality today can only be fully apprehended by pointing at evidence from the language, programs, infrastructures, relations, data, and technology that power structures control, manipulate, and hide. This contemporary postvisual condition is introduced by Trevor Paglen, commenting on the work of Harun Farocki, "wars are being waged through systems that are simply postvisual, or more accurately, systems whose imaging capacities exceed those of human eyes to the point of being invisible to them."[1]

Since the late sixties, artists have responded to increasingly tangled socio-political and technological developments. Representations of the modern reality of systemic complexity were initially questioned by Jack Burnham and Hans Haacke, who argued, "easel art can no longer convey the subtleties and complexities of the international business world...If you make protest paintings you are likely to stay below the sophistication of the apparatus."[2] Inherent limitations of objectivity and the representation of complex social issues were addressed by Martha Rosler as "inadequate descriptive systems"[3] for addressing evidence of intentions and contexts of reception as disguising devices, which Roland Barthes initially discussed as the "overconstruction"[4] of photography. These reflections brought to maturity the documentary category and, as Hal Foster noted recently, "this critique of the document is largely assimilated, and many artists have passed from a posture of deconstruction to one of reconstruction."[5] The tendency of evidentiary realist artists to show evidence is in effect about the impulse and urgency of reassembling fragments from our entangled and opaque reality and in doing so it reconciles with the original legacy of realism and documentary practices. As Rosalyn Deutsche noted, "today critical practices claiming the legacy of realism [..] explore the mediation of consciousness by representation and investigate the conditions of possibility of what is perceived to be 'real' at a given historical moment."[6]

In turn, the epistemological critique of the document is integrated with an investigation of the factual aspects of the subject matter. *Evidentiary Realism* considers the contexts of the sociopolitical, technical, and cultural infrastructures of complex systems that influence the perception and validation of truth and reality in an explicit empiricism of epistemic inquiry. The real can be seen only by simultaneously accounting for the multiple infrastructural signals, referents, relations, and processes of the various parameters that produce reality. It's with *Evidentiary Realism* that artistic research into systemic and structural apparatuses pushes the boundaries of what can be seen beyond sight.

Realism is enhanced

Beside the assimilation of epistemological examination, today realism in art is also enhanced by advancing technological and cognitive capability, which allows artists to capture, access, and process reality as never before. The technologies of detection and presentation provide easier, faster, and cheaper means to render, represent, and share relevant information. The relentless "technological turning point"[7] in media and science introduces novel forms of evidence to be used and discussed, while "the current wave of interactive and telematic technologies [..] enables users to access previously inaccessible data about complex (and often hidden) social relationships."[8] Artists can investigate and decode complexity through a wide range of material and techniques, ranging from high-resolution photo cameras, scanners, and satellite images to data-mining, hacking, leaks, social media content, open source intelligence, and archival or instant news items. These materials can now be computed on relational timelines and in databases correlated with geographic, architectural, biological, and financial data. Even the most complex black boxes are interrogated by counter black boxes programmed to illuminate the obscure artificial intelligence, high-frequency trading, and big data of our computational society. The asymmetry of the power of vision and knowledge is bound to be a pursuit of the technological field that will keep levelling itself.

The forums of presentation and legitimization have also expanded. Both evidence and artworks are shared over networks, and, in turn, are collectively discussed and verified. Citizen journalism, research, and criticism complement institutional and mainstream outlets in validating evidence-based work, while a broad audience acknowledges such evidence through a variety of distribution networks. As Eyal Weizman noted, "the protocols and languages of the forum will be reorganized around new aesthetic, material, and systemic demands. Forums are immanent, contingent, diffused, and networked; they appear, they expand and contract."[9]

Quantifiable, computable, and shareable documentary forms provide a sense of amplified realism. An unseeable reality appears to us as sharper evidence once it is intercepted and decoded in all its complexity. Enhanced realism in documentary art can be conceptualized as "forensic information," which here is broadly interpreted as in-depth analysis of media and content gathered from a variety of sources and techniques and combined with "forensics linguistics" to analyze modes of rhetoric, representation, and reception. Yet, the enhancement of realism in art goes beyond the use of tools, material, and knowledge available today. Realism can be achived only with independent studies and critiques of the social, economic, legal, and political contexts of institutional power. As Weizman stated, "forensis is forensics where there is no law, beyond State law."[10] The autonomy of the research is also inflected on the results of the works; "The outcomes of 'investigatory art,' like those of investigative journalism, have no legal authority but can act as an agent for change by creating public awareness that instigates action."[11]

Such politics of representation and presentation of evidence come into relation with the field of aesthetics. Giving significant artistic form to evidence is about articulating the intentions, outcomes, and contexts of the artworks; this is how evidentiary realist artists address the circumstances that produce their artworks—and truly enhance realism.

Realism of evidentiary aesthetics

Evidentiary works explore the aesthetics of secrecy, complexity, rhetoric, and the control of social, economic, and technological systems. The evidence is presented through a variety of artistic strategies: juxtapositions, ready-mades, reconstructions, abstractions, and compositions that reveal networks of relations, languages, operations, and infrastructures. Beyond the visual presentation, evidence is articulated with dialectical reflection and discourse on the subject matter and its representation. Yet evidentiary artworks do not make use of slogans or refer to the artist's subjectivity—the evidence presented is meant to speak for itself.

The aesthetics of *Evidentiary Realism* is often "post-spectacular," defined as "imagery characterized by its forensic look at the evidence of violence, which comes to stand in for what we don't see."[12] The process of investigation, the nature of the material, and the sensibility of the artists eventually transform the evidence into highly aesthetic visual works. However, this aesthetization of evidence differs from traditional documentary art. It can instead synthesize complex systems and make them accessible, catalyzing responses from the audience, who otherwise would not sense the evidence emotionally and visually—similar to how Laura Poitras describes her projects which, "both create an aesthetic experience and reveal information that evokes an emotional response."[13] Composing aesthetic and stylistic forms from evidence prompts the viewer to intimately sense the emotive elements invoked by the artists. With formal visual language and mediums, evidentiary realists intelligently engage with the formal qualities of the documentary tradition. As such, the artists are invested in how to convey evidence through abstraction, figuration, or commentary. Unseeable, fabricated, or bare evidence is portrayed within specific aesthetics, forms, and conceptual frameworks of visual art. For instance, "visual perspective and the spatial representation of complex systems"[14] were implemented in diagrammatic drawings by Mark Lombardi as a rigorous aspect and technique of visual art. The formal mediums of photography, film, drawing, painting, and sculpture used in evidentiary artworks provide a captivating means to transform the material of the investigation into evidence. The materialization of the intellectual, emotive, and intuitive artistic process creates physical evidence akin to the notion of "real evidence" in the legal field. Such "material evidence" are objects brought to court to perform proof and where the aesthetics for sensing, mediating, narrating, and presenting evidence play a judicial role. Similarly, physical artifacts, compositions, and installations assembled by evidentiary realist artists are objects articulating proof in the form of artworks.

Investigative aesthetics is an interdisciplinary artistic practice characterized by research and field work in human rights, war crimes, ecocide, political collusions, legal, and financial inequalities. Artistic research looks at the fabric of associations and chains of actions between people, environments, events, and things. Interrogating, seeking, finding, connecting, and inquiring into leaked and discovered evidence fuels the artistic process of making evidentiary artworks, which are created from the artist's sensibility, curiosity, and intuition. The artists often unveil realities already fully present in the world, as open secrets, or "leaks" from systems that are too complex and large to be completely hidden and undecodable. However, the detectable evidence might be still at threshold of visibility or disguised by secrecy and complexity. In all these cases, evidentiary works present the unintelligibility of evidence, or the connections among decoded hints, or refined details available to expose their meaning. Evidentiary realists purposefully challenge the detectability of complex systems to illuminate and enhance what can't be seen at plain sight and qualify as evidence.

Despite its agenda to expose the concealed real, *Evidentiary Realism* is not necessarily political art in classical terms. Its social function is inscribed in its own right. It questions the fundamental politics of representation itself with profound philosophical questions on art-making and its audience, role, and use in society. *Evidentiary Realism* enhances the tradition of the historical realisms in art, with artworks becoming advanced learning tools to build in-depth social knowledge and inquiry.

Realism returns

The return of reality prevails in an advanced capitalist society that increasingly pushes the planet to extreme social crises. The shift in the perception of the real-world and impulse toward realism in art can be exemplified at a time when nobody dares to openly deny climate change philosophically and scientifically. This return of reality has already been marked in several social crises, provoking the popular demand for truth and social justice. The opposition to the Iraq War, Occupy Wall Street, Wikileaks, Edward Snowden, the Panama Papers, Climate March, Black Lives Matter, and the recent resistance to Donald J. Trump and Brexit are among only the most evident signs of an intensification in acknowledging critical social issues and in valuing the exposure of the truth.

In art, this time of crisis is reflected through the expansion of the aesthetics of social engagement, socio-critical and protest art, interventionism, institutional critique, and *Evidentiary Realism* outlined here. Through a historical perspective, we can notice that the return of realist aesthetics naturally reflects times of social and economic crises. In fact, realism in art can be traced back to France in the aftermath of the nineteenth century revolutions, which compelled artists to reject Romanticism for realist depictions of famine, labor, and political turmoil. After this initial wave of realism, Impressionism emerged and elevated the personal over the social. This pattern of waves of aesthetics oscillating between prioritizing social or subjective reality emerged and it cycled again during the economic recession of 1930s, the post-war period, and the social unrest of the sixties and the seventies. We can infer that we are now moving through a new wave of realism in art after the last decades of the twentieth century, which were characterized by pop art, nihilism, and postmodernism. It is with the beginning of the twenty-first century that the social sphere and its representations are again pushed to the forefront of social inquiry.

Rooted in the critique of globalization, neoliberalism, and ecological destruction, the return of reality and the impulse towards realism in art can be traced to the aftermath of September 11, 2001. As Julian Stallabrass also noted, "the reawakening of documentary has been a product of the over-reach of neoliberal power, particularly [...] the launching of controversial wars, starkly dividing the globe into allies and enemies, and the violating democratic principles, thrust documentary in a renewed prominence."[15] The collapse of the Twin Towers signalled the decline of subjectivism in postmodernist and poststructuralist philosophies that prevailed from the late seventies to the nineties. The duplicity of reality, which Jean Baudrillard coincidentally identified in the Twin Towers,[16] turned into a monolithic reality as a harsh response to the attacks. In this time of history, the postmodern relativity of the real is gradually losing discursive influence, while the urgency of economic, social, and ecological crises has become dramatically concrete. Even in the so-called post-factual era, truth seems to be manufactured in unsophisticated modes: blatant falsehoods seem to be lauded as power of denial of evident facts. In post-truth, reality is denied by opposing it with authoritarian voices, which ultimately responds to the popular fear of the return of reality.

While the manifestation and mystification of political rhetoric has renewed its violence in different forms over the centuries, it is the popular peril of false information propagating online that makes fact-checking a common activity for most people. Nevertheless, humanity is approaching a critical stage of global crisis with climate change, neglected war crimes, mass surveillance, civil rights, and the freedom of speech, bringing a new theoretical revaluation of documentary art and the roles it plays within this social and political context. Similar to how the French Realists moved away from Romanticism, we now see the exhaustion of postmodernist relativism and its paradigm losing its representational relevance. At its apex, realist aesthetics may want to refuse subjectivity, ambiguity, allegory, and spectacle. Susan Sontag reminded us in 2002, "real wars are not metaphors."[17] As such, *Evidentiary Realism* reckons with a framework for a profound portrayal of contemporary times.

Notes:

1 Trevor Paglen, "Trevor Paglen on Harun Farocki," *Artforum*, Feb 2015.
https://www.artforum.com/passages/id=50135

2 Jack Burnham, *Recent Works: Hans Haacke*, exhibition catalog (Chicago: The Renaissance Society at the University of Chicago, 1979).
http://www.renaissancesociety.org/exhibitions/296/hans-haacke-recent-works/

3 Martha Rosler, *The Bowery in two inadequate descriptive systems*, 1974-1979.

4 Roland Barthes, "Shock-Photos," 1969.

5 Hal Foster, "Real Fictions: Alternatives to Alternative Facts," *Artforum*, April 2017.
https://www.artforum.com/inprint/issue=201704&id=67192

6 Rosalyn Deutsche, *Hans Haacke*, October Files 18, MIT Press, 2015.

7 Thomas Keenan, Eyal Weizman; *Mengele's Skull: The Advent of a Forensic Aesthetics* (Berlin: Sternberg, 2012).

8 Edward A. Shanken, "Investigatory art: Real-time systems and network culture"; November 22, 2012.

9 Eyal Weizman, *Forensic Architecture: Notes from Fields and Forums*, (Ostfildern: Hatje Cantz, 2012).

10 Eyal Weizman, "Forensis Is Forensics Where There Is No Law," *MetaMute*, Dec 16, 2014. http://www.metamute.org/editorial/articles/forensis-forensics-where-there-no-law

11 Edward A. Shanken, op cit.

12 Christy Lange, "The Limitations of Photojournalism and the Ethics of Artistic Representation," *Frieze,* June 2010. https://frieze.com/article/shooting-gallery

13 Laura Poitras, *Laura Poitras: Astro Noise*, (New York: Whitney Museum of American Art, 2016).

14 Carolyn Christov-Bakargiev, *Mark Lombardi*, (dOCUMENTA (13) (Ostfildern: Hatje Cantz, 2013).

15 Julian Stallabrass, *Documentary*, Whitechapel: Documents of Contemporary Art, (Cambridge: MIT Press, 2013).

16 Jean Baudrillard, *Simulations*, (Los Angeles: Semiotext[e], 1983).

17 Susan Sontag, "Real Battles and Empty Metaphors," *New York Times*, September 10, 2002.

Evidentiary Realism

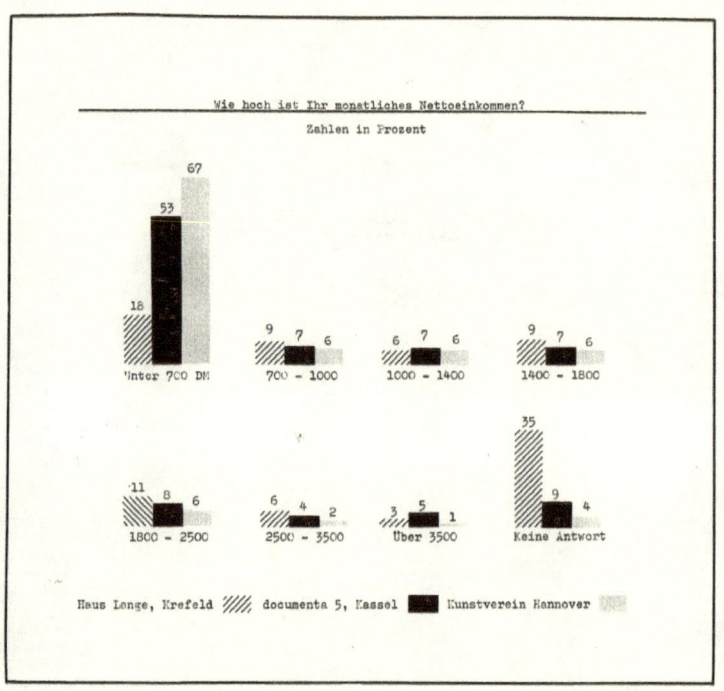

Comparison of 3 Art Exhibition Visitors' Profiles, 1972-76.
Hans Haacke

Ten silkscreen prints mounted on aluminum.
38,6 x 34,6 in. 98 x 88 cm.
Results of polls taken at Museum Haus Lange, Krefeld, 1972;
Documenta 5, 1972; Kunstverein Hannover, 1973.
Courtesy of the artist.

Comparison of 3 Art Exhibition Visitors' Profiles

by Hans Haacke

Comparison of 3 Art Exhibition Visitors' Profiles is a comparison of the results of three polls conducted in art exhibitions in Germany between 1972 and 1973. These surveys gathered answers to socio-political and demographic questions on the audience at the exhibitions. Questions on the visitors' political opinions were adjusted to the three different contexts, while the demographic questions remained the same. Each of the three polls posed twenty questions. The comparison was made between the answers to the nine questions that were identical at each of the three venues. While in Hannover and Krefeld the answers to the questions were tabulated by hand, at Documenta 5 in Kassel they were processed by the regional computer center. Intermediate results were posted during each of these exhibitions. The demographic questions concerned the visitors' age, profession, income, education, and relation to the art world. The socio-political questions inquired about their opinions on laws regarding abortion, the influence of churches on the country's affairs, the admission of members of Communist organizations to the civil service, and which political party would vote for. The comparison of polling results was produced for a solo exhibition at the Frankfurter Kunstverein in 1976.

Comparison of 3 Art Exhibition Visitors' Profiles correlates data to provide a comparative analysis as evidence of sociological conditions within their respective contexts. The participatory instruments of democratic political systems such as voting, demographic studies, and opinion surveys create information on the public and the parameters of social systems. The documents produced through such social engagement and information systems are presented with the visual language of data computation and integrated into a work of art.

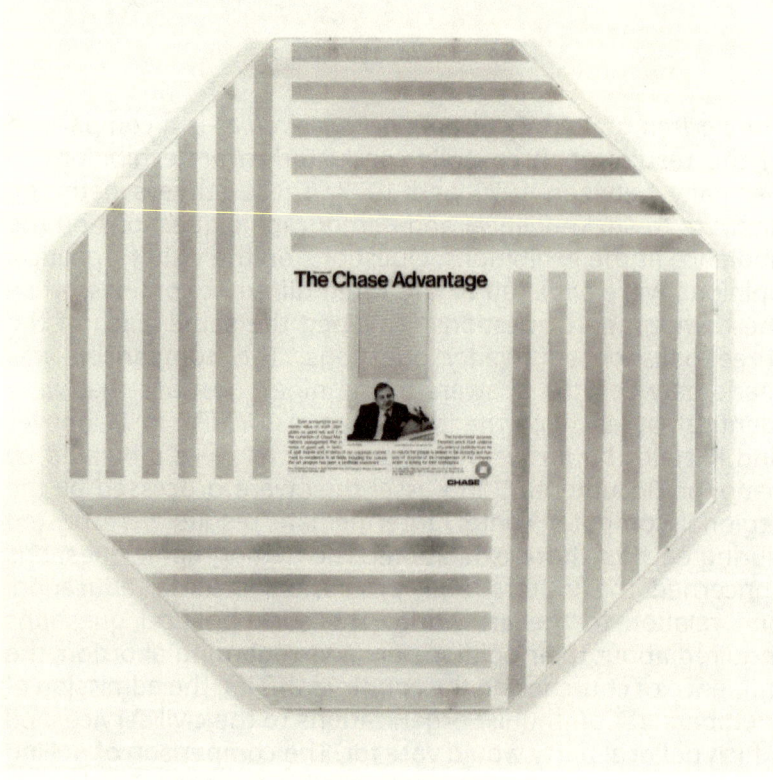

The Chase Advantage, 1976.
Hans Haacke

Screenprint on shaped acrylic plastic.
48 x 48 in. 121,9 x 121,9 cm.
Edition 3 of 6. Courtesy of the artist and Paula Cooper Gallery.
Photo: Steven Probert; copyright Hans Haacke and Artists Rights Society.

The Chase Advantage

by Hans Haake

The Chase Advantage is a composition of photos, graphics, and quotations. The hexagonal logo of Chase Bank serves as a frame for elements from an advertisement, two quotes, and the photo of a painting by Victor Vasarely above David Rockefeller at the time when he was chairman of Chase Manhattan Corporation. He also served twice as chairman of the board of the Museum of Modern Art in New York from the sixties to the nineties. Chase was a major financial supporter of the right-wing Manhattan Institute for Policy Research, with close ties to the CIA. The statement by David Rockefeller praising investment in the arts is juxtaposed with a quote from a book by Ivy L. Lee praising the manipulation of public opinions by means of publicity. John Davison Rockefeller Jr., father of David Rockefeller, hired Ivy L. Lee after the 1914 *Ludlow Massacre* where forty striking workers, including women and children, were killed by the Colorado National Guard in a coal mine that Rockefeller partially owned. Currently, David Rockefeller is the oldest living member of the family and he is Honorary Chairman at Museum of Modern Art in New York. In 2006, at 91 years old, he teamed up with former Goldman Sachs executives to form a fundraiser in support of Republican candidates.

The Chase Advantage exposes manipulative rhetorical devices by combining public statements and quotations as evidence. Juxtaposing, composing, and appropriating ready-made information reveals instrumental uses of art, language, and ideology. It points to the social complexity of a multiplicity of systems functioning simultaneously in economic, political, and cultural contexts. Imaginative analysis of verifiable facts is integrated with systems theory and aesthetics, together condensed into a work of fine art.

The Location of Power

by Lauren van Haaften-Schick

Give Yourself the Chase Advantage was the slogan used by Chase Manhattan Bank in the late 1970s. At the time Hans Haacke's work *The Chase Advantage* was made, the bank had been collecting art for display in its offices and as a company asset for over fifteen years, in addition to supporting numerous museum exhibitions, establishing itself as a force in the turn towards corporate sponsorship for art that had begun a decade prior.[1] By the mid-1980s North American museums had become dependent on major global corporations, trading "promotion for patronage,"[2] and today that practice is widely becoming the norm among art institutions throughout the world. Corporate logos and positivist slogans now regularly grace the walls of museum entrances, and their pervasiveness has become as deceptively neutral as the white wall itself. If these are the given conditions that artists must find themselves in if they are to attain visibility in art institutions, what strategies remain to insert a critique of the financial and art "apparatus" their work is threaded through?[3]

Hans Haacke's contestation of the framework and ideology of that apparatus proposes some ways that it might be undermined, exploited, and held accountable. One tactic is the artist's "devotion to factual accuracy,"[4] described by Benjamin Buchloh, Howard S. Becker, and John Walton as a strategy of providing irrefutable, publicly accessible information about the context the artist's work responds to and inhabits, resulting in the implication – though not a direct conclusion – of a theory "about the exercise of power in the art world."[5] Crucially, Haacke should not be imagined as a "political martyr";[6] instead, his work must be considered dialectical in its insistence on inhabiting the system and aesthetic of programmatic governmentality, and investigating all nodes that make up (to borrow the artist's term) the total "industry" of art.[7] For John A. Tyson, Haacke's method also possesses "a parasitic" capacity, wherein his works are able to "slightly reprogram their hosts, causing them to transmit politically charged messages," which constantly remind us of a "para-site" outside the literal frame, made visible through the work's insistence upon connecting content and context.[8] This potential for Haacke's works to "reprogram" their support systems is amplified by Rosalyn Deutsche's observation that his strategies can also be considered as transforming "aesthetic space into one where power [can] be questioned," and repositioning the art audience as "a public capable of giving itself the right to politics."[9] Within the right to politics is the right to insist on political fact becoming public knowledge, which Haacke's archeology of evidence demands.

Tracing the elements of the publicity rhetoric and commodity aesthetic appropriated in *The Chase Advantage* demonstrates this strategy in action. Surrounded by the graphic logo of the bank is David Rockefeller, who in 1976 was the Chairman of Chase Manhattan Bank and Vice Chairman of the Museum of Modern Art.[10] On the wall behind him hangs a painting by Victor Vasarely that belongs to the Chase art collection. [11] To Rockefeller's left we encounter a publicity statement attributed to him, claiming that for the bank's conviction in the "corporate commitment to excellence in all fields... the art program has been a profitable investment." On his right is a quote from the public relations consultant Ivy L. Lee, stating that the fundamental purpose of publicity policies must be "to induce the people to believe in the sincerity and honesty of purpose of the management of the company which is asking for their confidence." Lee was hired by John D. Rockefeller Jr. after the Ludlow Massacre of 1914, in which over forty striking coal miners and their families were killed in an armed assault; John D. Rockefeller was majority owner of the mining company.[12]All of this information—visual and textual—resides within a series of nested frames that telescope outwards once their linkages have been mapped in the mind of the viewer. The contours of the art object follow those of the bank's hexagonal logo, within which its slogan calls us to embrace "the Chase advantage," defined implicitly in Rockefeller's statement below promoting a philosophy that even intangibles can have a "money value." In the background, Vasarely's abstraction looms over the banker as an emblem of art's instrumentalization under late capitalism.

Haacke's formal mimicry of Chase bank's branding and publicity performs a subversive act of "paracitation," to borrow Tyson's term, quoting the corporation's recognizable visual identity in order to "interrupt flows of information and produce short-circuits – giving spectators pause for reflection."[13] Here Haacke's parody takes on an even sharper edge once we consider the total history encompassed within the pair of appropriated publicity statements and the sites and sources of their utterances. At their juxtaposition lies the history of violence against labor, and the capacity of capital to reduce anything—including aggression and "good will"—to an abstract value. Re-presenting the "truth" narrative advertised by corporate power back to itself, Haacke undertakes a "systemic and successfully executed project of delegitimation,"[14] reclaiming (partially at least) the public forum of art from the "managers" who preside over it, and demonstrating that social and political fact can be leveraged in order to demand accountability, in service of protecting democratic politics in an open agonistic sphere.[15]

Pointing to the corporate affiliations and financial ties of museums was introduced as a key strategy for Haacke in the work MoMA Poll of 1970.[16] Exhibited in the first room of the landmark exhibition Information at MoMA, the poll asked visitors to place a ballot in a "yes" or a "no" box recording their answer to the question of whether Governor Rockefeller's failure to denounce President Nixon's war in Vietnam would impact their vote for his reelection.[17] Governor Rockefeller, like his brother David Rockefeller, was a member of the museum's board of trustees at the time. As Deutsche has deftly mapped, David was a central figure in maneuvering bank and government power in the ensuing years, leading to the formation in 1973 of the Trilateral Commission, an organization whose goal was to bring about a new world order led by the liberal democracies of North American, western Europe, and Japan. One of the commission's reports considered the future "governability of democracy," and concluded that, following the political protests of the 1960s, financial and government hierarchical authority must be restored by "a return to passivity on the part of the people."[18] Now over forty years past this dawn of the "deep state," where democratic governments are themselves governed by the influence of major banks, Haacke's demand for public knowledge of the truth behind power rises in urgency. At the same time, the thick entanglements of art, financial, and political power have only increased in their complexity.

Today, JPMorgan Chase & Co. is the largest bank in the United States, with extensive international interests, $1,602,352M in Domestic Assets and $2,118,497M in Consolidated Assets.[19] President and CEO of the bank, Jamie Dimon, is an advisor in President Trump's Strategy and Policy Forum. Also in the Forum is Larry Fink, Chairman and CEO of BlackRock, Inc., the largest asset manager in the world, currently overseeing $5.15 trillion in assets; as of January 2017, $1 trillion of the funds managed by BlackRock are now under the custodianship of JPMorgan Chase.[20] Fink is on the Board of Trustees for the Museum of Modern Art, and in 2016 he received the David Rockefeller Award, presented annually by MoMA to "an individual from the business community who exemplifies enlightened generosity and effective advocacy of cultural and civic endeavors." In MoMA's 2006 expansion, the portion of the museum housing their exhibition spaces was named the Peggy and David Rockefeller Building. When on view, Haacke's works in MoMA's collection will be exhibited in that building. Returning to Deutsche and Tyson's observations concerning the potential for Haacke's work to claim a "democratic" sphere, made possible by its 'parasitic' inhabitation within the art institution and art industry, there is one more layer within this archeology of power relations that is worth exposing. Since 1971, Haacke has sold his work using *The Artist's Reserved Rights Transfer and Sale Agreement*, a contract written by curator/dealer of Conceptual art Seth Siegelaub and lawyer Robert Projansky that enables artists to retain a radically high level of control over the exhibition, reproduction, and resale of their work.[21] Copies of the Siegelaub-Projansky Agreement reside in various collections in the museum's archive holdings, and when MoMA acquired Haacke's work *The Solomon R. Guggenheim Board of Trustees* (1974) in 2011 as part of the Herman and Nicole Daled Collection, the museum became a signatory to its governing contract.[22] *The Solomon R. Guggenheim Board of Trustees* traces family memberships and corporate directorships of the

Guggenheim Museum and Foundation to reveal the political implications of their financial interests. The most extensive list of connections is tied to the Kennecott Copper Company, revealing that two museum trustees and one Guggenheim family member served on its board; At the time, the corporation controlled a large share of Chile's copper mines, and had been denounced by President Salvatore Allende for draining the country's resources before he was overthrown in a coup in 1973. The piece was created following the cancellation of Haacke's 1971 solo exhibition at the Guggenheim Museum in New York, which was censored on the grounds that three works concerning "real-time social systems"—two of which displayed publicly available information revealing the corruption of major New York real estate owners and slumlords—were inappropriately political for the museum's definition of art.[23] As Deutsche has observed, Haacke's presentation of the deeply interwoven relations between the managers of the museum and the forces of economic power behind major industry can be read as a direct challenge to the Guggenheim's assertion that the political has no place in an art museum. Instead, Haacke reveals that the inverse is irrefutably true: political and financial power is embedded within its total infrastructure.[24]

Perhaps the most enduring aspect of Haacke's overall strategy emerges as the network of power relations it exposes expand and shift over time, so that as the work circulates through the art institutional network it accumulates new layers of critique. MoMA's acquisition of the Daled collection (including Haacke's work) was made possible in part with funds from some of the most aggressive real estate developers in New York, leading us back to the original controversy spurring the piece. Here we find demonstrated the dialectical nature of this entire exercise: the project of reflecting power back to itself can take the form of a viral co-habitation with the subject of its critique, but endemic to that proximity is the risk of subsumption by the subject of that critique. [25] Yet stored away in files and boxes behind the museum's walls, the latent presence of the Siegelaub-Projansky Agreement accompanying *The Solomon R. Guggenheim Board of Trustees*, signed by Haacke and MoMA's representatives, serves as a reminder that claiming a right to politics may take many forms, though evidence of it may take time to unfold. As editions of The Chase Advantage are transferred or sold and re-sold, the Siegelaub-Projansky Agreement is the legal instrument that will record and confirm those transactions. Whether or not the work is exchanged, the specter of the Agreement covering *The Chase Advantage* maintains the work's total critique as residing not only in that which is reflected in its visible text and image, but in the mobilization of the total work as an instrument itself, capable of exposing and effecting the political and financial infrastructure as it accretes the marks of its movement through that system.

The author would like to thank Hans Haacke, Paolo Cirio, Imani Brown, Abram Coetsee, Kenneth Pietrobono, Annie Racugglia, and John Tyson for their invaluable comments.

Notes:

1. Brian Wallis, "Institutions Trust Institutions," in Hans Haacke: Unfinished Business, ed. Hans Haacke, Rosalyn Deutsche, and Brian Wallis (Cambridge, Mass.: MIT Press, 1986), p. 51.

2. Ibid., p. 53.

3. In an interview from 1972 Robert Smithson observed that artists are "alienated" from the value of their work, and that the focus of artists in the 1970s will turn towards "the investigation of the apparatus the artist is threaded through." Bruce Kurtz, "Conversation with Robert Smithson (1972)," in Robert Smithson, the Collected Writings, by Robert Smithson, ed. Jack D. Flam (University of California Press, 1996), 262–69. Quoted in Craig Owens, "From Work to Frame, or Is There Life After 'The Death of the Author,'" in Beyond Recognition: Representation, Power, and Culture. Berkeley: University of California Press, 1992, p. 122.

4. Benjamin. H. D. Buchloh, "Hans Haacke: Memory and Instrumental Reason," in Neo-Avantgarde and Culture Industry: Essays on European and American Art from 1955 to 1975 (Cambridge, Mass.: MIT Press, 2000), p. 205.

5. Howard S. Becker and John Walton, "Social Science and the Work of Hans Haacke," in Framing and Being Framed: 7 Works, 1970-75, by Hans Haacke (Halifax: Press of the Nova Scotia College of Art and Design, 1975), p. 150.

6. Buchloh, "Hans Haacke: Memory and Instrumental Reason," p. 206.

7. See generally: Hans Haacke, "Museums, Managers of Consciousness," in Deutsche et. al., Hans Haacke: Unfinished Business, p. 60. Also quoted in Craig Owens, "From Work to Frame, or Is There Life After 'The Death of the Author,'" p. 134.

8. John A. Tyson, "The Context as Host: Hans Haacke's Art of Textual Exhibition," Word & Image 31, no. 3 (July 2015): 213, 224.

9. Deutsche references Etienne Balibar's notion of the "right to politics" as "a right of all to constitute a social sphere and to put it at risk." ibid., p. 34. See: Etienne Balibar, ed., "Rights of Man" and "Rights of the citizen": The Modern Dialectic of Equality and Freedom', in Masses, Classes, Ideas: Studies on Politics and Philosophy Before and After Marx (New York: Routledge, 1994), p. 49.

10. In 1976 David Rockefeller held 4% of Chase's shares, and numerous other members of the Rockefeller family had major financial stakes in the company. Hans Haacke, "The Chase Advantage," in Deutsche et. al., Hans Haacke: Unfinished Business, p. 176.

11. Buchloh describes Vasarely as an example of an artist whose work has succumbed to the volatility of the art market. See: Buchloh, "Hans Haacke: Memory and Instrumental Reason," p. 204.

12. The mining company was the Colorado Iron and Fuel Company. Haacke, "The Chase Advantage," in Deutsche et. al., Hans Haacke: Unfinished Business, p. 176.

13. Tyson, "The Context as Host: Hans Haacke's Art of Textual Exhibition," p. 221.

14. Buchloh, "Hans Haacke: Memory and Instrumental Reason," p. 226. I follow Chantal Mouffe's description of agonism as a democratic form not of consensus but of conflict, debate, and strategic alliance. See: Chantal Mouffe, "Deliberative Democracy or Agonistic Pluralism," Social Research; New York 66, no. 3 (Fall 1999): 745–58. John A. Tyson also applies this concept to the work of Haacke in Tyson, "The Context as Host: Hans Haacke's Art of Textual Exhibition," p. 213.

15. Rosalyn Deutsche, "Hans Haacke and the Art of Not Being Governed Quite So Much," p. 30, 33.

16. Text of MoMA Poll (1970): "Question: Would the fact that Governor Rockefeller has not denounced President Nixon's Indochina policy be a reason for you not to vote for him in November" "Answer: If 'yes' please cast your ballot into the left box, if 'no' into the right box.

17. Rosalyn Deutsche, "Hans Haacke and the Art of Not Being Governed Quite So Much," p. 30, 33.

18. Wells Fargo & Co ranks 2nd with $1,686,690M in Domestic and $1,740,819M in Consolidated Assets. See: "Insured U.S.-Chartered Commercial Banks That Have Consolidated Assets of $300 Million or More, Ranked by Consolidated Assets as of September 30, 2016." (Federal Reserve Statistical Release, September 30, 2016). (Accessed March 16, 2017).

19. Emily Glazer and Justin Baer, J.P. Morgan to Become Custodian for $1 Trillion in BlackRock Assets, Wall Street Journal, January 25, 2017, sec. Markets.; Occupy Museums, "Debtfair: A Project of Occupy Museums," 2017. At the time of this writing, JPMorgan Chase is also the subject of critique in Debtfair, a project of Occupy Museums, on view within the Whitney Biennial 2017, of which Chase is a sponsor. The project collects and presents data on the financial debt conditions of artists and how those networked relationships connect to the financial industry's control of culture and the economy.

20. For additional writing on the Siegelaub-Projansky Agreement and Haacke's use of the document see: Maria Eichhorn, The Artist's Contract, ed. Gerti Fietzek (Cologne: Verlag der Buchhandlung Walther König, 2009).; Lauren van Haaften-Schick, "Contract as Form and Concept: The Siegelaub-Projansky Agreement in Art and Law," in Intellectual Property and Visual/Digital Culture (Association for the Study of Law, Culture, and the Humanities, Eighteenth Annual Conference, Georgetown University Law Centre, Washington, DC, 2015).; Jeanine Tang, "Future Circulations: On the Work of Hans Haacke and Maria Eichhorn," in Provenance: An Alternate History of Art, ed. Gail Feigenbaum and Inge Reist (Los Angeles: Getty Research Institute, 2013), 173–96. John Tyson, "Hans Haacke: Beyond Systems Aesthetics," (Ph.D. Dissertation, Emory University, 2015), pp. 308-309). The Agreement is available online through Primary Information

21. Herman Daled assisted Siegelaub with the French translation of the Agreement, and with its distribution in Europe.

22. Haacke's controversial works were Shapolsky et al. Manhattan Real Estate Holdings, a Real-Time Social System, as of May 1, 1971, 1971; Sol Goldman and Alex DiLorenzo Manhattan Real Estate Holdings, a Real-Time Social System, as of May 1, 1971, 1971; and a visitor's poll that would tabulate their responses to demographic questions,

resulting in sociological information about the status and class make up of exhibition attendees.

23. This argument was central in the public defense by museum leadership concerning the cancellation of Haacke's 1971 exhibition at the Guggenheim Museum in New York City, and the censorship of Haacke's Manet-PROJEKT '74 at the Wallraf-Richartz-Museum/Museum Ludwig in Cologne in 1974. See: Rosalyn Deutsche, "Property Values: Hans Haacke, Real Estate, and the Museum," in Deutsche et. al., Hans Haacke: Unfinished Business, pp. 20–37.; Hans Haacke and Edward F Fry, Hans Haacke: Werkmonographie (Köln: M. DuMont Schauberg, 1972); Hans Haacke, "Provisional Remarks," (1971) in Institutional Critique: An Anthology of Artists' Writings, ed. Alexander Alberro and Blake Stimson, 2009, 120–28.; Hans Haacke, "Manet-Projekt '74," in Deutsche et. al., Hans Haacke: Unfinished Business, pp. 119–34.

24. On the notion of artist's contracts, certificates and documents as "virus" and "parasite" within art institutions and publications see: Ingrid Schaffner et al., eds., Deep Storage: Collecting, Storing, and Archiving in Art (Munich; New York: Prestel, 1998).; Josh Takano Chambers-Letson, "Contracting Justice: The Viral Strategy of Felix Gonzalez-Torres," Criticism 51, no. 4 (2010): 559–87.; Tyson, "The Context as Host: Hans Haacke's Art of Textual Exhibition" (2015).

Hans Haacke (b. 1936, Germany) is best known for exploring the aesthetic and representational qualities of systems and their relations to socio-political conditions. His commitment to realism can be traced to his early interest in empirical phenomena. He began his career in Germany as a painter. He then joined the ZERO Group, an avant-garde European art movement. In 1961 and 1962, with a Fulbright grant, he was affiliated with the Tyler School of Art of Temple University in Philadelphia. After a year in New York he returned to Cologne, Germany for two years. In 1965 he moved permanently to New York, where he continued to pursue his interest in physical phenomena, working directly with physical systems and then also with biological systems. In 1969 he began working with social systems. That year, in his solo exhibition at the Howard Wise Gallery in New York, in addition to other works, he presented *News*, a printer delivering the newswire of UPI live into the gallery, as well as *Gallery-Goers' Birthplace and Residence Profile, Part 1*.

In 1971, he investigated two major real-estate corporations in Manhattan. One of the two, *Shapolsky et al. Manhattan Real Estate Holdings, a Real-Time Social System, as of May 1, 1971*, was the largest in slum areas of Manhattan (predominantly East Village, Lower East Side and Harlem). The other, *Sol Goldman and Alex DiLorenzo Manhattan Real Estate Holdings, a Real-Time Social System, as of May 1, 1971*, was the largest private real estate holding, mostly in upscale areas of the borough of Manhattan. It included the Chrysler Building. These works are seen as representing a significant moment in the history of art for their portrayal of a specific factual and systemic reality by way of a functional and informative mode of representation. Haacke continued making artworks integrating "institutional critique" and social commentary. He taught at The Cooper Union in New York for 35 years, from 1967-2002, and is currently Professor of Art Emeritus.

Hans Haacke was included in five editions of Documenta, 5, 7, 8, 10, 14, Kassel; the Venice Biennale, 1976, 1978, 1993, 2009, 2015; at the biennials of Tokyo, 1970; São Paulo, 1985; Sydney, 1990; Johannesburg, 1997; Gwangju, 2008; Sharjah, 2011; Mercosul, 2013; and the Whitney Biennial, New York, 2000. He shared with Nam June Paik the *Leone d'Oro* for the German Pavilion at the 1993 Venice Biennale. He had solo exhibitions at Museum Haus Lange, Krefeld, 1972; Museum of Modern Art, Oxford, 1978; Stedelijk Van Abbemuseum, Eindhoven, 1979; Renaissance Society, Chicago, 1979; Tate Gallery, London, 1984; New Museum of Contemporary Art, New York, 1986; Centre Pompidou, Paris, 1989; Fundació Antoni Tàpies, Barcelona, 1995; Museum Boijmans Van Beuningen, Rotterdam, 1996; Portikus, Frankfurt, 2000; Serpentine Gallery, London, 2001; Generali Foundation, Vienna, 2001; Deichtorhallen, Hamburg and Akademie der Künste, Berlin, 2006; Museo Nacional Centro de Arte Reina Sofía, Madrid, 2012; 4th Plinth, Trafalgar Square, London, 2015.

Lauren van Haaften-Schick (b. 1984, U.S.) is a curator and writer from New York. She is currently working on a PhD in the History of Art and Visual Studies at Cornell University, and is the Associate Director of the Art & Law Program in New York. Research interests concern the artistic appropriation of legal theories and tools; artists' labor, property, and moral rights; art historical issues in law; and critical forms of circulation, with a focus on early conceptual art, institutional critique, and the work of Seth Siegelaub.

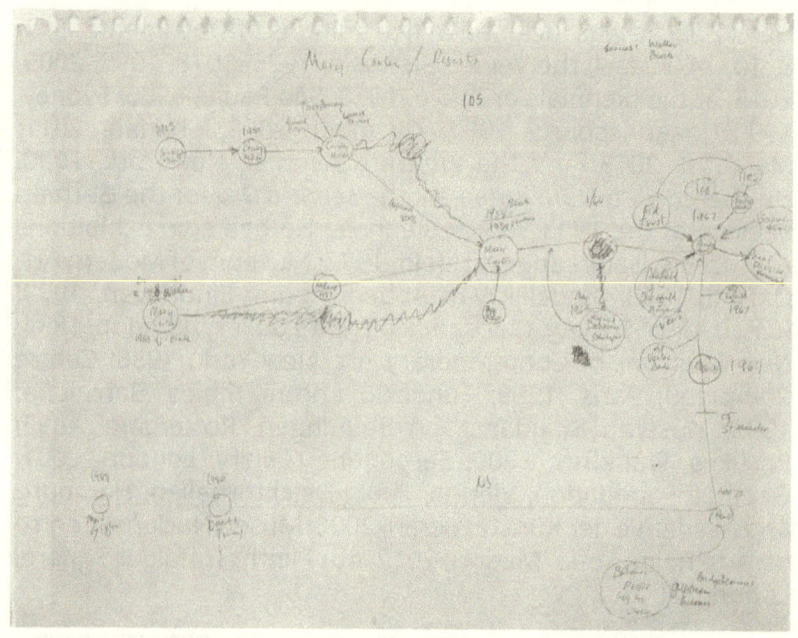

Mary Carter Resorts Study, 1994.
Mark Lombardi

Ballpoint pen ink on paper.
11 × 14 in. 27,9 × 35,6 cm.
Courtesy of Pierogi Gallery, NYC.

Mary Carter Resorts Study

by Mark Lombardi

Mary Carter Resorts Study is a preliminary sketch of a diagram for mapping connections between organized crime, politicians, and intelligence agencies through the Mary Carter front company and casinos in the Bahamas. Mary Carter Paint Company, which operated a national chain of paint stores, was to function as a covert CIA money-laundering operation. The company was set up in the early 1950s by then CIA director Allen W. Dulles and New York Governor Thomas E. Dewey, political functionary in the so-called Rockefeller Republicans. In 1958–59, Dewey and a number of associates used CIA funds to buy the Crosby-Miller Corporation (headed by Dewey friend James Crosby). After the merging of the companies, the name was changed to Resorts International in 1968, and it ran casinos in the Caribbean. Jim Crosby was an alleged CIA frontman who later founded a private security company called Intertel, whose clients included the late Shah of Iran and late Nicaraguan dictator Somoza. When Crosby died, his family sold the Resorts International to Donald J. Trump, in 1987. In his own memoir, *The Art of the Deal*, Trump proudly described how he bought his first casino interests when he purchased 93 percent of the Resorts International gambling concern.

Mark Lombardi's work investigates evidence of social, political, and economic transactions. Depicting evidence in the form of networks evokes the interconnection of information as a primary material of investigation. The linking, tagging, archiving, and cross-referencing of fragmented information is used as a creative practice to decode highly complex social and financial relationships. The resulting detailed and delicate geometrical drawings provide a nuanced understanding and immediate visualization of the complexity of global power structures.

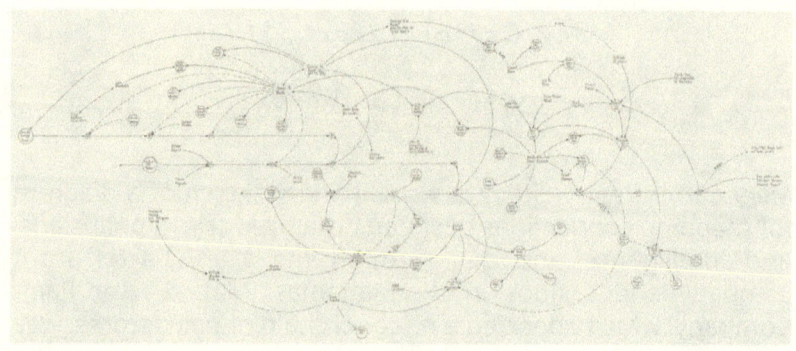

George W. Bush, Harken Energy, and Jackson Stephens, c. 1979 - 91, 4th version, 1998.
Mark Lombardi

Graphite on paper.
18.5 × 43 in. 47 × 109.2 cm.
Courtesy of Robert Tolksdorf

George W. Bush, Harken Energy, and Jackson Stephens, c. 1979-91, 4th Version

by Mark Lombardi

George W. Bush, Harken Energy, and Jackson Stephens, c. 1979-91 charts financial transactions and political collusions among the U.S. presidents Bush Junior and Senior, Osama Bin Laden's family business, global banks and tycoons. After college George W. Bush founded the Texas oil company Arbusto Energy and in 1979 began to raise 4.7 million. The capitalization was brokered by his businessman acquaintance James R. Bath, who managed a portfolio worth millions of dollars for wealthy Saudis, including Sheikh Salem bin Laden, brother of Osama bin Laden and the oldest son of Mohammed bin Awad bin Laden, founder of the Saudi Binladin Group, one of the largest construction companies in Saudi Arabia. In 1980, Bath also invested in Arbusto through a Cayman Islands company called Cotopax, which was controlled by his client Sheikh Khalid bin Mahfouz, a powerful banker in Saudi Arabia who was later accused of funding Al Qaeda. Eventually, the Bush's Arbusto oil venture failed and the company was merged with Spectrum 7 Energy Corp in 1984, which was subsequently acquired by Harken Energy in 1986 through a stock swap. Bush Junior joined Harken as a director and was given 212,000 shares of Harken stock. In 1988, Harken Energy Corp signed a lucrative contract with the government of Bahrain. The financial transaction, signed by both Jackson Stephens, an Arkansas tycoon, and Abdullah Taha Bakhsh, a Saudi real estate investor, was carried out through the Bank of Credit and Commerce International (BCCI), which was a large global bank involved in money laundering scandals for drug cartels, terrorist organizations, and international secret services. BCCI was largely controlled by Jackson Stephens and Sheikh Khalid bin Mahfouz. Beyond arranging this transaction for Bush Junior, Stephens also backed Jimmy Carter and Bill Clinton. Finally, in 1990, George W. Bush sold his Harken stock with a profit of 848 thousand dollars. Both FBI and Homeland Security agents scrutinized this drawing after the 9/11 attacks.

Edges of Evidence: Mark Lombardi's Drawings

by Susette Min

At first glance, Mark Lombardi's *George W. Bush Harken Energy and Jackson Stephens* c. 1979-91, (1998) looks like a flow chart or systems designs engineering plan with its curving arcs and shooting arrows from different nodes pointing to other modules in various shapes and forms. Inscribed in these "circles of influence" in neat block handwriting are the names of world leaders, bankers, arms dealers, intelligence agents, drug smugglers, oil sheikhs, corporations, mobsters, terrorists, dictators, and government officials. Lombardi's drawing could be approached as an austere portrait of the global power elite. In contrast to the drawing's systematic appearance and schematic clarity, the combination of thick and thin, dotted and connected lines, semi-circles and other graphic notations also represent timelines of shadowy deals, exchanges of dirty money, and hidden power relations that span over the course of decades.

The recent charges against Paul Manafort, President Trump's former campaign manager, and Rick Gates, lobbyist and business associate of Manafort, of conspiring against the United States and laundering money elicit a feeling of déjà vu and history repeating itself. One wonders how Mark Lombardi would have rendered this recent theater of influence peddling and consolidation of power between the Trump Administration and Russia, and more urgently, what it would have revealed. Already, in *Mary Carter Resorts Study* (1994), Lombardi revealed Trump's connections with organized crime and the world's wealthiest elite. Once a manufacturer of house paints, in the 1960s, Mary Carter Paints became Resorts International, a lucrative casino enterprise, that was also known to serve as a front company for the CIA. In 1987, Trump won controlling stake in Resorts International, only to give it up a year later in exchange for ownership of the Trump Taj Mahal Casino Resort (Atlantic City, NJ);[1] a flailing venture, fraught with charges of breaking all types of violations, including anti-money laundering rules.[2] The latest leaks documented in the Paradise

Papers disclose multiple conflicts of interest between Trump and his ties with a number of cosmopolitan elites including his own presidential cabinet who have engaged in offshore dealings, contravening his populist pledge to bring back trillions of dollars back to the U.S. by way of curbing aggressive tax evasion schemes. Any kind of sentencing and incarceration of the Trump Administration will be a big feat, but also small compensation, for the years of unchecked global corruption and money since the advent of the First Gulf War and the election of George H.W. Bush. Put another way, the current chaos wrought on the geopolitical landscape by the Trump administration threatens to obscure not only the profits gained by the Bush Family by way of clandestine deals with the bin Laden family, the Saudi royals, Saddam Hussein, the Bahrain government, and BCCI, but also how wars and accountability are produced and erased under these motley regimes.[3]

George W. Bush Harken Energy and Jackson Stephens c. 1979-91 trenchantly reminds us of this era by framing key clusters of names, including George W., with palm tree-like fireworks, that explode rhythmically left to right along the page, on three horizontal tiers, embedding him and others within multiple flows and dimensions of global capital. A narrative of this web of connections might read as follows (to contrast with its effect on the viewer in the timeline), beginning in the 1970s: In 1977, one of the initial investors for George W. Bush's first oil exploring company, Arbusto Energy, was James Bath, a representative for Salem bin Laden, oldest son of Mohammed bin Laden, founder of Saudi Binladin Group, the largest and oldest construction company in Saudi Arabia, and half-brother of Osama bin Laden. Due to a combination of factors—the end of Arab oil embargos and reduced domestic consumption of crude oil—Arbusto struggled, and in 1984 merged with William DeWitt Jr.'s Spectrum 7 Energy Corp. of Ohio; a company rumored to be in the business of creating tax shelters rather than exploring oil. On the brink of bankruptcy, Harken Energy, a distressed oil properties specialist, bought Spectrum in the mid 1980s, and invited George W. to be on its board of directors. Harken was led at the time by Alan G. Quasha, an attorney with no experience in the oil business, but who had financial connections to Compagnie Financiere Richemont AG (a Swiss based investment company), Harvard Management Company, and Aeneas Venture Corp, and whose father was also an attorney and close supporter of president Ferdinand Marcos. And despite the company having consistent financial troubles through the 1990s, in which the company suffered millions of dollars in losses, investors continued to pour money into Harken, such as Salem bin Laden and Jackson T. Stephens, founder of one of the largest investment banking firms of Wall Street, and one of the richest people in Arkansas, who secured $25 million dollars from the Union Bank of Switzerland, a subsidiary of Bank of Credit and Commerce International (better known as BCCI). By investing money into Harken, Sheikh Abdullah Taha Bakhsh, former director of Saudi Arabia's income tax department, and Khalid Bin Mahfouz, a shareholder at BCCI, were able to purchase not only a stake in the company, but also power and foreign influence in the United States.

Central to all these transactions was BCCI, which closed in 1991, with losses estimated at more than $20 billion-dollars, bringing with it the collapse of one of the largest criminal enterprises in history. The U.S. prosecution of BCCI and its laundering of money, engagement in extortion, and blackmail, facilitation of income tax evasion, and financing of illegal arms trafficking and global terrorism was criticized in the press at the time as sloppy and sluggish, due in part to stonewalling by then Assistant Attorney General Robert S. Mueller (now special counsel to oversee the investigation of Trump and his ties to Russian officials). Doing very little to follow up on critical errors made by the Justice Department, and attributing culpability of BCCI's long list of serious misconduct to smaller banking institutions and mid-level BCCI officials, Lombardi's drawing hints at a different accounting of not only wrong doing, but how the different relations depicted influenced and/or circumscribed foreign policy.

Drawing on and departing from the tradition of history painting and its moral imperatives, Lombardi's drawings offer less a clash of civilizations than an updated way of representing imperialism and global capital, framing key players by a set of lines that radiate from their names. What first began as a way to make clear the links and cross-references of bits and pieces of information about various bank frauds told by a lawyer-friend in combination with publicly accessible documents and information he found during this research, Lombardi's flow charts became according to Devon Golden, an "aha!" moment in which the artist found the form to match his curiosity and interest in the world of corporate finance and government corruption.[4] By probing various connections and following different money trails, Lombardi's narrative diagrams are sketches of his thought process, but also part of a long legacy of institutional critique, one that goes beyond the links between money, art, and politics. It's not hard to discern the political connections Lombardi's work has with the likes of Hans Haacke's *Shapolsky, et al. Manhattan Real Estate Holdings, A Real-Time Social System, as of May 1, 1971* (1971) and Fahrettin Örenli's *Conspiracy Wall* (2014), and the stylistic similarities with Beth Campbell's *My Potential Future Based on Present Circumstances* (1999-present) and Janet Cohen's *Location and Time Drawings* (2006-2007). What is singular and remarkable about Lombardi's understated drawings is its currency in demystifying the relationships between corporations and countries, petro-capitalism and U.S. geopolitical objectives.

In contrast to searching on Google about George Bush and Harken Energy—a telling of events through linear narrative form—Lombardi's mark making process entails gleaning and paring down the details of the numerous financial transactions, asset transfers, vested sales, and bail outs—translating and transcribing the circulation of money, by way of dotted lines—and inscribing on paper a combination of dense lines and reticulate webs that lead to a catalogue or register of names. Here, viewers might be reminded of Don DeLillo's *The Names* (1982) whose protagonist, James Axton, narrates a tale of risk analysis along with his interactions with corporations and intelligence agencies. Whereas the novel gets bogged down in plot twists and hidden secrets in its presentation of concealed networks of influence, Lombardi's tale of this parallel subculture appears light, almost translucent, rendering in drawing what DeLillo attempts to show through fiction: "...a naked structure [of] ... abstract structures and connective patterns. A piece of mathematics."[5] I refer to DeLillo here, because he shares with Lombardi an ambitious attempt to push through the spectacle and the "sightlines of living history." DeLillo, in his attempt to push the limits of literary realism, felt he "had to reduce the importance of people. The people had to play a role subservient to pattern, form, and so on." In contrast, in Lombardi's narrative structures, the interactions of his international cast of characters become part of a larger syntax and design related to capitalism's stranglehold on government and society, which at the same time is hinted at, but never directly articulated, leaving his drawings open-ended, defying closure and fixed readings.

Wary of how knowledge comes to us in the form of decontextualized information, Lombardi's drawings, taken with his index cards, which he used to synthesize his understanding of a particular event or person and was part of his artistic practice, resist the way this overflow of knowledge can erode the ability to know what's really going on, i.e. the truth.[6] It is almost impossible not to infer in his drawings, an underworld of political intrigue, but rather than throwing furious amounts of data on the page as proof of such activities, Lombardi converts this array of knowledge into different versions that I want to suggest cumulatively become edges of evidence. Resisting the positivist demand for literal connections of these different relations, Lombardi deploys as formal elements the material relevance and associations of these once obscure power relations to other forms of evidence, the latter contingent on the observer to uncover and make the connections. The clean and accessible two-dimensional presentations of Lombardi's narrative structures meet our cultivated desire and pleasure for beautiful objects to be orderly and symmetrical, inviting the viewer to come up close and scrutinize one of his drawings by following the different lines and looking "obliquely at the edges of things, where they come together with other things."[7]

His drawings also share a clean quality of information design in which his landscapes of seedy insider trades, duplicitous bailouts, and shady family connections are able to escape the "flatland" of uninspired data presentation, to borrow a term from Edward Tufte, but with space on the page to spare. Lombardi's work shares much with the tenets of Tufte's *Envisioning Information* (1990) with regard to form, as well as a common agenda—"Tell the truth. Show the data in its full complexity. Reveal what is hidden...Let the viewers make their own discoveries"—and perhaps even an aversion to technology.[8] By, as Tufte puts it, "removing as much visible weight as possible from the display and [playing] up the eloquence of empty space," Lombardi's drawings are unmistakably works of art that, at the same time, interpellate viewers of his work into witnesses.[9] His artistic practice merges aesthetics and ethics by calling upon the observer-cum-witness to take on the responsibility of etching these traces deep into the surface, to resist repression or erasure of such forms, and follow up on fleshing out this evidence and associations of the various relations depicted in order to challenge this profane vision of American democracy as well as to act and restate the demand for public knowledge and nuanced details that point to larger complex realities and multi-faceted truths.

Notes:

1 Russ Buetnner and Charles V. Bagli, "How Donald Trump Bankrupted His Atlantic City Casinos, but Still Earned Millions," *New York Times, June 11, 2016:* https://www.nytimes.com/2016/06/12/nyregion/donald-trump-atlantic-city. html (last accessed November 14, 2017)

2 Jim Zarroli, "Looking Into Trump Campaign's Russia Ties, Investigators Follow the Money, *NPR*, May 15, 2017: https://www.npr.org/2017/05/15/528486988/ investigators-looking-into-trump-campaigns-russia-ties-follow-the-money (last accessed November 14, 2017)

3 Alan Friedman and Amy Goodman, "The Reagan-Saddam Connection: We Create These Monsters and When It's Not Convenient We Cover Them Up," June 9, 2004: https://www.democracynow.org/2004/6/9/the_reagan_saddam_ connection_we_create (last accessed November 14, 2017)

4 Frances Richard, "Toward a Diagram of Mark Lombardi," footnote 3. Richard's rich and insightful essay is a must-read about Lombardi's artwork and practice. http://www.whale.to/c/mark_lombard3.html

5 Don DeLillo, "An Interview with Don DeLillo (and Thomas LeClair/1982)," Edited by Thomas DePietro, *Conversations with Don DeLillo* (Jackson: University of Mississippi, 2005) 11.

6 The 14,000 three-by-five inch index cards include condensed bullet-point entries on multinational corporations, individuals, and his own friends, organized in alphabetical order. The notecards are now part of the permanent collection at the Museum of Modern Art in New York.

7 Clifford Geertz, "The Near East in the Far East," *Life Among the Anthros and Other Essays*, edited by Fred Inglis (Princeton: Princeton University Press, 2010) 183.

8 Michael H. Martin, "The Man Who Makes Sense of Numbers," *Fortune*, October 27, 1997.

9 Edward Tufte quoted by Robert Hobbs in *Mark Lombardi: Global Networks* (New York: Independent Curators International, 2003) 43.

Mark Lombardi (b. 1951 – 2000, U.S.) was an American neo-conceptual artist who specialized in drawings that document financial and political frauds by power brokers. His diagrammatic drawings resemble a mind-map and depict systemic entanglements behind significant financial and political scandals. In the *New York Times*, Roberta Smith referred to Lombardi as an "...investigative reporter after the fact." In the aftermath of September 11, 2001, FBI and Homeland Security officers inquired about viewing Lombardi's works.

Mark Lombardi's work has been exhibited widely in the U.S. and internationally and was the subject of a traveling, one-person retrospective, *Mark Lombardi: Global Networks* organized by ICI and curated by Robert Hobbs (Herbert F. Johnson Museum of Art, Cleveland Museum of Contemporary Art, The Drawing Center, 1998-2005), and has been included in exhibitions at the Museum of Contemporary Art Leipzig, 2008-2009; Musée du Louvre, Paris, 2015; S.M.A.K., Ghent, 2015; MoMA, New York, 2011; the Whitney Museum, New York, 2005; dOCUMENTA (13), Kassel, 2012; and the Sharjah Biennial, 2011, among many others. His work is included in the permanent collections of MoMA, the Whitney Museum, and Jewish Museum in New York; The Smithsonian Art Museum, Washington, D.C.; and the Reina Sofia Museum in Madrid, along with many private collections. He is represented by Pierogi gallery in New York.

Susette Min (b. 1968, U.S.) is a curator and Associate Professor at the University of California, Davis where she teaches Asian American studies, art history, cultural studies, and curatorial studies. Min has curated exhibitions at The Drawing Center, NYC; Whitney Museum of American Art; Berkeley Art Museum; and the Asia Society.

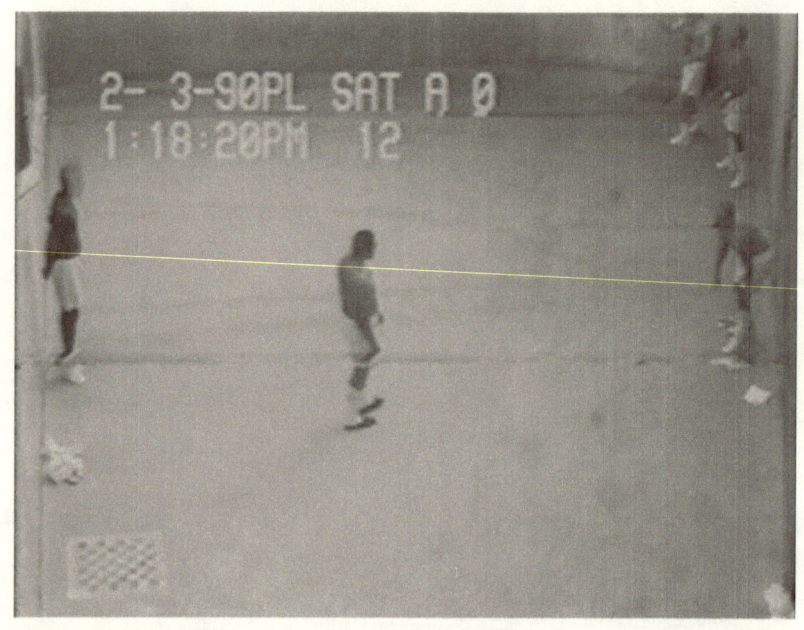

I Thought I Was Seeing Convicts, 2000.
Harun Farocki

Digital video projection, one channel, 23 min., BetaSp.
Courtesy of Harun Farocki GbR.

I Thought I Was Seeing Convicts

by Harun Farocki

I Thought I Was Seeing Convicts is a video containing images from a maximum-security prison in Corcoran, California. The surveillance camera shows a yard where the prisoners are allowed to spend half an hour each day. Fights often break out between inmates, guards call out warnings and fire rubber bullets, and if the convicts do not stop fighting, the guards will shoot live ammunition. This experimental documentary tackles the brutal realm of prison surveillance through the use of split-screen, voice-over commentary alternating with silence, and explanatory infographics. The video installation presents complex imagery from practices of watching and being watched, control, and the gaze throughout private and public spaces.

I Thought I Was Seeing Convicts narrates evidence of surveillance and prison abuse. The use of found footage and archival images manifests the evidence through a video documentary. The work's filmic language explores the nature of infrastructural and technical devices that produce intensive surveillance and social control, while the narration illustrates the significance of the images by commenting on the video sequences in the work.

I Thought I Was Seeing...

by Jaroslav Anděl

This essay examines the video installation *I Thought I Was Seeing Convicts* by Harun Farocki in the context of the exhibition *Evidentiary Realism* and in a broader context of how the attitude to concepts such as evidence, data, and facts has been changing. The premise of the essay is that the development of modern media and, more recently, of digital technology has been transforming the perception of the above-mentioned and other related terms.

Over the past four decades, Harun Farocki analyzed the central role that modern media plays in the late capitalist system more consistently than any other artist. I will argue that there is a certain parallel between our shifting relationship to media (manifested, for instance, in the declining trust in the mass media and statistical evidence) and the trajectory of Farocki's work. Farocki's critical stance had been anticipating rather than reflecting this shift, while providing valuable insights about the impact of mechanized and digitized vision on the construction of social and political subjectivity and its moral implications.

Farocki explored the use of images in contemporary society, including manufacturing, business, education, advertising, retail, propaganda, pornography, entertainment, prison, and war. He paid special attention to the growing presence of mechanized vision and its infiltration into every nook and corner of everyday life. In this respect, *I Thought I Was Seeing Convicts* complements works on other topics, for instance, on retail architecture and military training. Farocki took interest in Michel Foucault's ideas about modern institutions and his oeuvre can be regarded as an artistic parallel to the French philosopher's writings.[1]

In his influential book *Discipline and Punish*, Foucault brought attention to Jeremy Bentham's prison project called the Panopticon and argued that it created a new regime of visibility which informed other modern institutions.[2]

The idea of Panopticon is based on the belief that maximum visibility influences the behavior of those being watched and thus enables maximum surveillance and control. The possibility of being watched creates inhibition and conditions behavior. The Panopticon principle is ubiquitous in modern visual technologies, being constantly perfected through digitization. Hence the Panopticon has become the metaphor of today's surveillance society.

The etymology of the word "panopticon" reveals a moral component behind it and historical connections which make it suitable for a symptomatic reading.[3] Derived from from the Greek "pan" [all] and "opticon" [observe], the word belongs to the same family of words which refer to vision (for instance, "evidence" from the Latin root words "vid" [see] and the Indo-European "weid"). The notion of light represents another important etymological reference. These terms gained a new prominence and specific connotation in the period of the Enlightenment, whose very name explicitly foregrounds this reference, indicating that the Panopticon is a poster child of the Enlightenment.

The Age of Enlightenment is also called the Age of Reason, which suggests that "light" in the word "Enlightenment" means the "light of reason." This became a popular phrase by signaling a moral as well as an epistemic impetus, both morality and rationality. [4] It also implies a potential tension between them though. In addition, it entails the dualism of the light and the dark, and thus moral, ontological and epistemological dualisms which inform the development of modern philosophy and science, for instance, in the dichotomy of subject and object and the mind and body dualism.[5]

The rationalization of vision in the invention of linear perspective in Italian Renaissance led to the invention of various mechanical and optical devices and instruments, including camera obscura, and paved the way to the rise of modern subjectivity and individuality.[6] Renaissance painters applied Euclidean geometry to construct pictorial space and standardized their construction by using a single vanishing point, effectively linking empirical observation with mathematics. This application of geometry represents an early step in the mathematization of nature, a long-term trend which brought about the rise of modern science and technology, including technologies of mechanized vision and most recently the computer and digitization.[7]

Though these connections might seem too general with regards to Farocki's work, they have direct implications for his core interests and concerns. For instance, born out from the moral and rationalist arguments of the Enlightenment, the Panopticon connects directly to their separation in mechanized vision manifested in *I Thought I Was Seeing Convicts*. In other words, there is a trajectory from the mathematization of nature in mechanized vision to Auschwitz and mass killings in the war, which is the point Farocki made in a few works.[8]

It is no coincidence that the terms which became hallmarks of modern science and then everyday expressions of modern life, such as evidence, data, information, facts, and documents, emerged or gained their current meaning mostly at the very dawn of the Age of Reason, i.e. in the early 1600.[9] This is the time when linear perspective was already the codified mode of pictorial representation in the western world. The invention of new optical instruments such as the microscope and telescope then started to extend empirical observation on microscopic and macroscopic scales. It was the same period in which René Descartes made his fundamental distinction between subject and object as res cogitans and res extensa, thought and extension.[10]

Also in the 17th century, mathematics applied to the study of population gave rise to statistics. Like the invention of linear perspective two centuries earlier, statistics as a new science of producing and analyzing data originated in standardization and the use of mathematical techniques. In the post-Westphalian era, it enabled the state to aggregate data on a large scale and create a picture of the nation as a whole. Statistics thus became a powerful instrument in the development of nation states and their centralizing power.[11]

This short overview suggests that three clusters (first, concepts, ideas, codes; second, instruments, technologies and media; third, socio-political institutions and subjectivities) are connected in feedback loops in which all clusters are mutually interdependent. How does the recent evolution of these interdependencies and Harun Farocki's video installation *I Thought I Was Seeing Convicts* fit in this nexus? The ethos of his work is grounded in the conviction that specific codes, technologies, and media aren't value free but are situated and/ or situate themselves in specific relationships in the existing socio-political order and that the role of the artist is to uncover these entanglements.

To achieve this goal, Farocki is using a CCTV footage from a high-security prison in Corcoran, California accessed through the Freedom of Information Act (FOIA) by a civil rights organization. He then mixes it with another found footage in double projection. Farocki thus reframes the original footage in several ways: first, by showing and editing footage from different cameras which wasn't intended for public viewing; second, by mixing it with another found footage; third, by inserting his comments, and finally by using a rather enigmatic title *I Thought I Was Seeing Convicts*. The title comes from Rossellini's film *Europe '51* in which the character played by Ingrid Bergman notices workers and says: "I thought I was seeing convicts."[12] The title is thus Farocki's acknowledgement of Foucault's ideas as well as of the tradition of two important topics, factory and prison, in film history.[13]

Farocki's insistence on the belief that images are implicated in the way power operates in contemporary society is most developed in his concept of operational image, i.e. images produced by machines not to be seen but to do something.[14] He developed this concept in the early 2000s and introduced it in the video installations *Eye/Machine I* (2000), *Eye/Machine II* (2001), *Eye/Machine III* (2002) and *Ausweg/Way* (2005). The idea is also present in *I Thought I Was Seeing Convicts*, as the last couple of sentences in Farocki's description of this work indicate: "The pictures are silent, the trail of gun smoke drifts across the picture. The camera and the gun are right next to each other. The field of vision and the gun viewfinder fall together..."[15]

Together with other uses of digitization and algorithms, operational images as the upshot of mechanized vision are now producing data of a different order and magnitude, and thus changing our attitude to evidence, data, facts, information. The glut of data and information does often create more confusion and disruption than clarity, and sometimes generates distrust and disbelief when it opens new opportunities for manipulation and disinformation. There seem to be an emerging notion that is seeping into the public consciousness, notably that data are not innocent, that they are also operational, i.e. produced by specific subjects and specific protocols for specific purposes, often not transparent or not known at all. Data are not indifferent entities but actors which may interfere in social and physical reality by shaping new political subjectivities.

The mathematization of nature in its current phase triggers the crisis of modern institutions, including political institutions associated with liberal democracy. The ideal of mathesis universalis advanced by Descartes in the 17th century materializes now in the way algorithms direct our lives, challenging the status quo and forcing us to rethink our institutions and safeguard the fundamental principles of freedom and social justice, public knowledge, and public argument. In this respect, Harun Farocki is a role model for artists and citizens alike.

Notes:

1. In this context, the following passage from Farocki's text *Written Trailers* is revealing: "I once travelled to a prison construction site in Oregon with an architect who was employed by an office with several thousand architects. He told me about a certain Bentham and his ideas about the Panopticon which were being applied to this building. He had never heard about Foucault or about all the subsequent discourses in which Bentham's idea had been read symptomatically and not as a practical proposal." Harun Farocki, Written Trailers, in:

Antje Ehmann, Kodwo Eshun (ed.), Harun Farocki. Against What? Against Whom?, Koenig Books, London / Cologne 2009, pp. 220-242.

2.   Michel Foucault, Discipline & Punish: The Birth of the Prison. Vintage Books, New York, 1995, pp. 195–210.

3.   See the Note 1.

4.   William B. Ashworth, *Light of Reason, Light of Nature. Catholic and Protestant Metaphors of Scientific Knowledge, Science in Context*, Volume 3, Issue 1, April 1989, pp. 89-107, DOI (Published online: 26 September 2008).

5.   For an instructive account of this topic, see Bruno Latour, 'Do You Believe in Reality?' News from the Trenches of the Science Wars, in: Bruno Latour, Pandora's Hope. Essays on the Reality of Science Studies, Harvard University Press, Cambridge, Mass., 1999, pp. 1-23.

6.   See William Mills Ivins; Jean Pelerin, On the rationalization of sight, with an examination of three Renaissance texts on perspective, Da Capo Press, New York, 1973.

7.   For a discussion of the early stage of this development, see Geoffrey Gorham (ed.), The Language of Nature: Reassessing the Mathematization of Natural Philosophy in the Seventeenth Century, University of Minnesota Press, Minneapolis, 2016.

8.   "My starting point now was the impending mass destruction through nuclear weapons. Hardly anyone responded to this attempt to relate Auschwitz to the current armaments situation. I worked on both versions (Bilderkrieg/Images-War, 1987; Images of the World and the Inscription of War, 1988) for about two years, mostly at the editing table." In: Harun Farocki, *Written Trailers*, Also, see *Dietrich Leder's note on Bilderkrieg Images-War*, (1987).

9.   See the following excerpts from the Online Etymology Dictionary entries Evidence (v.): Meaning "ground for belief" is from late 14c.; that of "obviousness" is from 1660s and sticks closely to the sense of evident. Legal senses are from c. 1500, when it began to oust witness. Also "one who furnishes testimony, witness" (1590s); hence turn (State's) evidence. Data (n.): 1640s, classical plural of datum, from Latin datum "(thing) given," neuter past participle of dare "to give". Fact (n.): Main modern sense of "thing known to be true" is from 1630s, from notion of "something that has actually occurred," "to support by documentary evidence" is from 1711. Document (v.): 1640s, "to teach;" meaning "to support by documentary evidence" is from 1711.

10. Descartes, R. (1641) Meditations on First Philosophy, in The Philosophical Writings of René Descartes, trans. by J. Cottingham, R. Stoothoff and D. Murdoch, Cambridge University Press, Cambridge, 1984, vol. 2, pp. 1-62.

11. William Davies, *How statistics lost their power – and why we should fear what comes next*. The Guardian, January 19, 2017.

12. "I had to deliver an outline and called it Ich glaubte Gefangene zu sehen, because I had just read the English edition of Deleuze's Unterhandlungen (Negotiations) where he quotes Ingrid Bergmann from Europa 51, saying: "I thought I was seeing convicts. "Harun Farocki, *Written Trailers*. In the context of the Evidentiary Realism exhibition, it is worth noting that Roberto Rossellini was a key figure of Italian neorealism, a national film movement after World War II.

13. "Because I spent half the year in the US I wanted to make films there too. A curator of a museum in New York asked me to produce something. I proposed an examination of the depiction of prisons in film and video, a study like Workers Leaving the Factory." In: Harun Farocki, *Written Trailers*, Farocki refers to the film Prison Images he made in 2000.

14. "Beginning with my first works on this topic (Eye/Machine, 2001), I have called such images, which are not made to entertain or to inform, 'operative images.' Images that are not simply meant to reproduce something but are instead part of the operation." Harun Farocki, War Always Finds a Way, Gagarin, 21 (2010), pp. 60-72.

15. Installation view and credits *I Thought I Was Seeing Convicts* (official page of the artist).

Harun Farocki (1944 – 2014, Germany) was a Berlin-based filmmaker, artist, and curator. Harun Farocki developed his own unique style of non-narrative-filmmaking concerned with understanding, reflecting and confronting modern society. Since 1966 Farocki produced, wrote, and directed more than 100 short and feature-length films for television and cinema, mostly documentaries, experimental and essay films, that analyzed social realities with a precise use of moving images that always included the political and sociological context involved in the creation of imagery.

His long list of credits since then includes over a hundred productions for video and cinema, the authoring and editing of the influential *Filmkritik* and numerous gallery and museum shows. His writings include *Speaking about Godard*, 1989; *War I Media I Art*, 2011. His summer 2011 retrospective at the MoMA, *Images of War (at a Distance)*, was the first comprehensive exhibition of his work in the U.S. In the 90's he was visiting professor at the University of California, Berkeley, and since 2006 he was full professor at the Academy of Fine Arts Vienna.

Jaroslav Anděl (b. 1949, Czech Republic) is a conceptual artist, photographer, art historian, curator, and pedagogue. He studied photography at FAMU, 1967–72, and art history at Charles University in Prague, 1969–73. He received his PhD from Charles University in Prague in 1982. Andel is the former director of the National Gallery in Prague's Museum of Modern Art, the founding artistic director of the DOX Centre for Contemporary Art in Prague, 2008-2015, the founder and director of the interdisciplinary serendipity research program at the Agosto Foundation in Prague, the author and co-author of more than 40 books and exhibition catalogues.

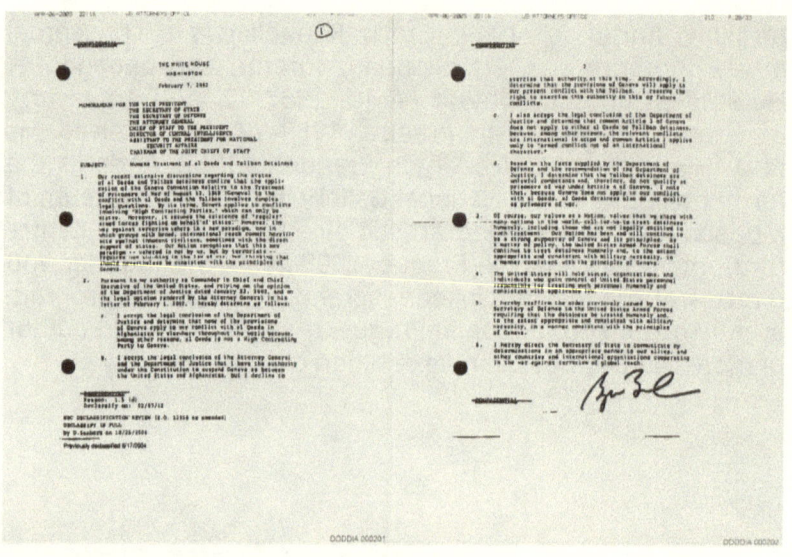

THE WHITE HOUSE 2002 GREEN WHITE, 2006.
Jenny Holzer

Oil on linen, two elements.
33 × 51 in. 83.8 × 129.5 cm.
Copyright Jenny Holzer / Artists Rights Society (ARS), NY / VG Bild-Kunst, Bonn,
2017. Courtesy of Sprüth Magers.

THE WHITE HOUSE 2002 GREEN WHITE

by Jenny Holzer

THE WHITE HOUSE 2002 GREEN WHITE is a painting of a memorandum signed in secrecy by President George W. Bush on February 7, 2002. The document was not declassified until June 2004. It legally legitimated the use of torture on prisoners of war seized in response to the September 11, 2001 attack and during the military operations in Afghanistan and Iraq. On October 11, 2001, a U.N. High Commissioner asked the U.S. and its allies to ratify obligations to the Geneva Convention against torture. Consequently, lawyers at United States Department of Justice, CIA, and White House argued that that the Geneva Conventions were inapplicable, giving ground for the use of torture and avoiding future persecutions under international laws and the U.S. federal War Crimes Act. On January 25, 2002 a White House Counsel memorandum to President Bush argued that the War on Terror required new interpretations of old paradigms of the law of war. The letter signed by George W. Bush stated that "[...] none of the provisions of Geneva apply to our conflict with Al Qaeda in Afghanistan or elsewhere through the world because, among other reasons, Al Qaeda is not a High Contracting Party to Geneva" and "I determine that the Taliban detainees are unlawful combatants and, therefore, do not qualify as prisoners of war under Article 4 of Geneva." This order created a new category of detainees, legally considered neither prisoners nor accused persons, but who had lost all legal status and held no rights. Eventually, the letter justified the "enhanced interrogation" torture methods on suspects initiated in August 2002 by the Office of Legal Counsel of the Attorney General, which were revealed in the "Torture Memos" after the scandals of the Abu Ghraib and Guantanamo detention centers. The artwork is part of the *Redaction Paintings* and *War Paintings* series with reproductions of legal rulings, memos, planning maps, diplomatic cables, interrogation records, autopsy reports, and handwritten notes from detainees.

THE WHITE HOUSE 2002 GREEN WHITE makes visible the legal and bureaucratic means of war. Unclassified and redacted documents as sources of evidence are utilized as forensic legal analyses of the structural secrecy and impunity of the military. The documents transformed into paintings draw attention to the materiality of the raw origin of the hidden bureaucratic violence and let the viewers experience it personally. The hand-painted canvases turn the abstract visual and verbal logic of protocols into detailed contemplations of war stories and the suffering to which they testify.

Can We See Torture?

by Joshua Craze

The memorandum that Jenny Holzer has painted in *THE WHITE HOUSE 2002 GREEN WHITE* is one of hundreds of documents that collectively constitute the archival record of America's War on Terror.[1] These documents are often heavily redacted. Over the last decade, they have been slowly released into the public record following Freedom of Information Act requests made by the media and organizations such as the American Civil Liberties Union (ACLU). For journalists and researchers like myself, these heavily redacted documents are crime scenes, and we are the detectives. Hidden amid the black of the redactions are the facts we have pieced together to reveal the story of the American government's use of detention, extradition, and torture. The very forms that are enabled by the memorandum Holzer painted were signed in secrecy by president George W. Bush on February 7, 2002.

In our investigations as researchers, the redactions themselves are obstructions that hide the truth. Their materiality disappears from news articles and reports, as redacted documents are digested and turned into sources of information. Journalists have to write about content, not absence, and describing redactions is outside their purview. No matter how opaque the redactions make the document, the journalists' end product is the same: four hundred words of precise prose that puts the redacted document's revelations in context. Words and narrative replace the mysteries of dealing with documents that are often more absences than presences. It is through such articles that the public gains access to the redacted documents. For although these documents are in the public realm, most of the public has not seen them: there are too many documents, and we have too much to do. Making sense of them is a task left to specialists. The public reads reports of torture in the newspaper, shakes its head in disgust or nods in agreement, and goes about its day. We read only the summarized content and not the redactions, which remain hidden in the documents.

As long as I have been reading these documents, Jenny Holzer has been painting them.[2] In painting them, Holzer removes the documents from the media cycle and turns them into objects of contemplation. Her work refuses the journalistic reduction of these documents to mere sources of information and insists that there is something to be seen in the redactions themselves. Instead of filling gaps in our understanding, the paintings replicate the omissions of the documents. In newspaper articles, accounts of detainee abuse are always placed into frameworks of meaning: Were human rights violated? Can torture be justified by ticking time-bomb scenarios? Is waterboarding really torture? Holzer's paintings suspend these questions and insist that, despite all we know about the War on Terror, we have yet to understand. If the redacted documents that Holzer paints make the truth invisible—a series of heavy black marks on paper, obscuring dates and names—then Holzer's paintings of these documents make this invisibility visible and ask us to dwell in it.

Her paintings thus take a position inverse to that of the US government, which asserts that these documents are nothing but content. This attitude is exemplified by the government's response to the ACLU's decade-long struggle to force the disclosure of approximately 2,100 images showing the abuse of prisoners in Afghanistan and Iraq. As of the beginning of November 2017, the government has released only 198 of these photographs.[3] Bad things happened, the government says. They *happened*. There's nothing to see here. For the government, all these documents are written in the past tense: they are merely sources of information about events that no longer have a hold on the present. Yet people linger in front of Holzer's paintings, despite assurances that the stories of the War on Terror now belong to the past. It is striking that so many of the people visiting her exhibitions of these works react as if the paintings were the documents themselves. Discussions around the artworks are as often about the details of the US detention program as they are about the texture of the paint. For many viewers of Holzer's work, this is the first time that they have seen such documents, though what they are viewing are paintings on a gallery wall. It is only when the documents have been transformed into painting that they become visible as documents and are not reduced to sources of information only comprehensible to specialists. It is important to be precise about what one encounters in these paintings. No one goes to an art gallery to connect the dots in their understanding of the War on Terror. Holzer's paintings are not a total history, and the documents she paints are fragments of an already-redacted documentary record. Rather, what one encounters, when staring at her paintings, is the form of the documents themselves. The stories that the media publishes about the War on Terror can be horrifying, but they are comprehensible. An arrest. Detention. Torture. The subjects have names. The reasons for their detention are evaluated. There is a quote from the White House press secretary.

Holzer ruptures these narratives by letting the documents speak. In some, names are redacted, while in others, only lines of speech remain, cut away from any recognizable subject. The identities of the characters of the documents are often unknown and act out scenes that are variously painful, terrifying, and absurd, but that have no referent. When I first looked at Holzer's paintings, I scrambled to contextualize them and give names and places to the scenes unfolding in the artwork. It was a mistaken attempt. Context dulls the impact. One's work, in front of the paintings, is to be an absurdist journalist—to find meaning and significance in the documents as images.

The real characters of the paintings are the documents themselves. Holzer cites their sentences and, in so doing, decontextualizes them, allowing the viewer to encounter them on their own terms, outside a media narrative that reduces the stories of the detainees to figures in the calculus of national security. Bureaucratic reports and detainee testimonies alike stand in front of us, demanding to be looked at by a world that would otherwise too quickly pass them by.

Holzer turns words into images so we can read them, as if for the first time.

NOTES:

1 I wrote a longer essay on these documents for the New Museum's Temporary Center for Translation (Summer 2014). See Joshua Craze, *A Grammar of Redaction*: http://www.joshuacraze.com/exhibitions/ (last accessed November 14, 2017)

2 I wrote a longer essay on Jenny Holzer's redaction paintings, which takes up some of the themes of the present piece. See Joshua Craze, *In The Dead Letter Office*, in *Jenny Holzer: War Paintings*, ed. Thomas Kellein (Cologne: Walther König, 2015), pp. 13–21.

3 Eliza Relman, *Pentagon Releases 198 Abuse Photos in Long-Running Lawsuit. What They Don't Show Is a Bigger Story*, February 5, 2016: https://www.aclu.org/blog/speak-freely/pentagon-releases-198-abuse-photos-long-running-lawsuit-what-they-dont-show-bigger (last accessed August 16, 2016)

Jenny Holzer (b. 1950, U.S.) is an American neo-conceptual artist. Her main practice is text-based work, and the public dimension is often integral to the delivery of her work. In the late 1970s, she devised nearly 300 aphorisms or slogans called *Truisms*, which play on commonly held truths and clichés printed on posters and disseminated throughout New York City. Her work developed with the creation of longer texts through her light projections on landscape and architecture. Her practice has revealed ignorance and violence with humor, kindness, and courage.

Jenny Holzer's work is widely exhibited internationally. Recent solo exhibitions include MASS MoCA, North Adams, 2017; Pinchuk Art Centre, Kiev, 2017; Phoenix Art Museum, 2016; Neue Nationalgalerie, Berlin, 2011; and Fondation Beyeler, Basel, 2010. She has participated in group exhibitions at the Whitney Museum, New York, 2015; Hayward Gallery, London, 2013; Martin Gropius Bau, Berlin, 2012; Serralves Museum of Contemporary Art, Porto, 2011. Holzer received the *Leone d'Oro* at the Venice Biennale in 1990; the World Economic Forum's Crystal Award in 1996; and the Barnard Medal of Distinction in 2011. She holds honorary degrees from Williams College, the Rhode Island School of Design, The New School, and Smith College. She lives and works in New York.

Joshua Craze (b. 1982, UK) is a writer from London. He is currently a Harper Fellow and Collegiate Assistant Professor at the University of Chicago. As a journalist, he is a fellow at The Nation Institute for Investigative Reporting, where his work on American national security was cited in a Senate inquiry. He is also a researcher on South Sudan with Small Arms Survey, and his publications with that organization have broken a number of major news stories on South Sudan. In 2014, he was a UNESCO Artist Laureate in Creative Writing. He was educated at the universities of Oxford and Amsterdam, L'École des Hautes Etudes en Sciences Sociales, and he has a Ph.D. in Sociocultural anthropology from the University of California, Berkeley.

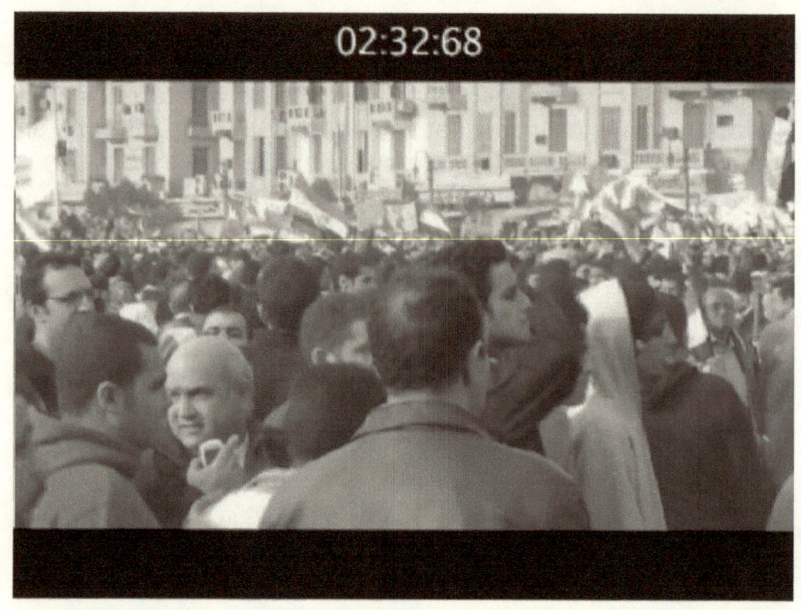

The Video Diaries, 2011.
Khaled Hafez

Digital video, one channel, 5:30 min., digital file.
Courtesy: Khaled Hafez and Mercusol Biennial.

The Video Diaries

by Khaled Hafez

The Video Diaries documents the artist's personal moments that he lived during the Egyptian revolution in January and February of 2011. The three-split screen of a synchronized identical timeline intertwines video footage that the artist captured, stock footage from broadcast media agencies, TV material, social media clips, and portraits of acquaintances. The footage of collective doing, revolting, and repression is assembled to create several parallel narratives that combine media-propagated imagery and direct first hand experience. The original music score created for the work adds intimacy and nostalgia as a tribute to political figures and personal acquaintances who died during the riots.

The Video Diaries portrays narrative structures of social turmoil through evidence from collective, mediatic, and personal memory. It incorporates video footage and still images from news feeds and online material as a hybrid form of primary document shared on worldwide networks. The visuals created from real-time-real-life footage assembled on a synchronized timeline presents the attempt to reconstruct intimacy from the depersonalization of social upheaval and its media representation.

The Magma of Reality

by Nicola Trezzi

There are two opposite ways to approach Khaled Hafez's *Video Diaries* (2011). The first and probably most tempting one, is to immediately bring the context to the forefront, to provide information that will clarify the kinds of images that we experience. If we take this path, we should immediately explain the various sources that the artist *appropriated*—a term that in the language of the Western history of art echoes a specific moment in time and space—in order to create this work. We should scrutinize what has been taken "as it is"—a video readymade if you wish—and what has been manipulated. However, the word manipulation here definitely leaves behind its etymology "mani" [hands] in order to refer to a digital manipulation, although digital also comes from "fingers"—whether through editing, special effects, music, etc. Last but not least, this approach would have to consider the political aspect of this work, the connection to the so-called "Arab Spring" and specifically the demonstrations in Egypt. It would be a very easy, fruitful, and informative analysis of a document capturing a recent chapter of our tumultuous present, its turmoil and its instability. Despite how fruitful this possibility might be, we must understand that Khaled Hafez's *Video Diaries* is first and foremost a work of art. As a work of art we must approach and understand it through the filters of creativity, authorship, signature, and labor.

As a creative act, the making of *Video Diaries* brings the aforementioned historical events to a different level of consideration and understanding. The filter of creativity here performs in a specific way due to the fact that what we see in the work is a mix between video material that has been taken—appropriated by the artist—as it is and rearranged and video material that has been manipulated by the artist. To be completely precise, both kinds of materials have been manipulated, but while the found material—footage taken from different media outlets—has been "softly" manipulated through the act of editing, the "new material"—the portraits—

have been visibly manipulated by altering the way these images come to us. Here again we understand how this work is imbued with a cut-and-paste attitude that links surrealism, automatism, collage, and the history of video art.

As the author of this work, Khaled Hafez takes full responsibility for the content and form of *Video Diaries*. At the same time, due to the nature of the materials employed in the work, we might assume that the artist is interested in a more complex form of authorship, a form that is connected to the notion of multiplicity, of shared economy (or struggle), of comradeship, and community. The structure of the work and the treatment of the materials once more reveal a double, or perhaps triple, position, that the artist simultaneously adopts. In the portraits of his comrades, to which this work is dedicated, Hafez's exhibits a strong sense of authorship. At the same time, the decision to portray relevant figures in Egyptian society, protagonists of a specific time in history, can make us believe that Hafez is using his position as an author and artist to bring other authors to the forefront. Therefore, although the images have been heavily altered, they seem to have their own status: holograms of heroes brought to us through Hafez. In the other materials, the rearranged footage from different media outlets, the authorship of the artist, is apparently less visible but in fact more strong, due to the fact that Hafez applies the notion of détournement here. Through his decision to re-edit, mix, and re-contextualize these materials, the footage is born again as a new creature, a sort of "new(s) Frankenstein." The third position, a suspended one, resides in the possibility of some of the materials being actually shot by the artist rather than a media outlet. Following the history of art, we could argue whether this part of *Video Diaries* is a collage of photographs taken by the other people (authors, artists, reporters, people demonstrating on the street using their phones) or by the artist.

As a work of art, *Video Diaries*' signature behaves according to the rule of the field. At the same time, we must also consider three elements that add complexity to Hafez's signature. The first element is connected to the appropriated material. Through using materials shot by someone else, whether through claimed authorship or in clear anonymity or lack of authorship, the artist superimposes his signature onto several others: that of the camera man shooting for the news, the people shooting in order to witness their presence, etc. The second element is the dedication to specific people, which comes at the end of the work. If we analyze *Video Diaries* as a traditional work of art, we will see that there are other signatures alongside that of the artist and this is in fact an act perpetuated by the artist himself, who is using this work to acknowledge people close to him. The final element is the double "function" (or dysfunction) of *Video Diaries*: on one a hand work of art, on the other a document. In fact, due to the material employed and appropriated, this work of art can serve not only as a mysterious and enigmatic "thing" whose sole "function" is to make us think and to trigger our mind and imagination; it also serves as a document of a specific moment in time and space, a historical moment for Egypt, the Middle East, and for the entire world—and by consequence for humankind. As paradoxical as it might seem, this work oscillates between being a tool and being its opposite; being functional and lacking any function; serving a cause and at the same time avoiding any possible goal. This is not surprising since Hafez's practice has already investigated issues that are opposite with each other, creating works that are oxymora.

Labor here plays a very special role. Because *Video Diaries* is both a work of art and the documentation of a historical moment, the labor behind it can be classified in different ways: either as the unique work of an artist or as the work of somebody who tries to narrate a very important chapter in the history of humankind through a mix of images and music. Furthermore, it must be taken into consideration that the artist plays a contradictory role. Not only because of the double context in which this work can exist—the field of art and that of documentary—but also because due to the material taken it becomes more complex to decipher the so-called "division of labor" in a work as such. In other words, due to the fact that this work includes images broadcasted by the media and often charged with propaganda, alongside more intimate first hand experiences documented by the people, including the artist himself, *Video Diaries* is the result of different kinds of labor. This labor is performed by different kinds of people who are united and edited by the artist—again through labor. In a mix, full of contradictions, done through different registers, originally presented and distributed quite differently, *Video Diaries* prompts us to reflect upon the complex nature of the reality surrounding us, a reality that art doesn't try to explain, to illustrate, or even to document, although it might use the language of documentation; rather, art tries to unfold it in order to make it more complex rather more easy to explain and understand; more obscure, rather than shedding light on this topic or that topic.

Due to this specific nature, this work can actually be considered a contemporary triptych. This word connects us to the history of painting, since usually the word "triptych" is used to define "a picture or relief carving on three panels, typically hinged together side by side and used as an altarpiece." This association, as bizarre as it might appear, actually makes a lot of sense, especially because of the choice of images and the way they have been treated. If we look, deeply and carefully at the faces animating this work of art, we realize how painterly they are, how their expressions can bring direct connection to certain paintings. As a continuation of the kind of approach we have taken so far, *Video Diaries* does not have so many elements that are not common to a triptych painting from the early renaissance. They both have a strong relationship to beauty, although its beauty might appear to us as grotesque, unbearable, and full of mistakes. They both document a specific moment in history, although they do it as complementation to the main channels for building history. Last but not least, they exist, as we said, in a specific moment in time and space (Egypt, 2011) but, at the same time, their goal is to go beyond these coordinates, to use this fraction of history in order to stir our imagination and perception of a reality that is ever more magmatic.

Khaled Hafez (b. 1963, Egypt) explores the complex nature of identity and the factors that shape it through painting, photography, installation, interdisciplinary art, video, and film. With a focus on his native Egypt, Hafez traces the amalgamation of cultural elements that have surfaced over the last five decades, as the country has experienced significant socioeconomic changes, increased militarization, and intense periods of political upheaval.

Hafez has participated in the Venice Biennale, 2017, 2015, and 2013; Moscow Biennale, 2015; Mercusol Biennial, Porto Alegre, 2011; Manifesta 8, Murcia, 2010; Cairo Biennale, 2010; and Sharjah Biennial, 2007. His work has additionally been exhibited in institutions like MOCA, Japan, 2012; Tate Modern, London, 2007; MuHKA Museum of Art, Antwerp, 2007 & 2011; New Museum, New York, 2010; and the Centre George Pompidou, Paris, 2010 & 2012. Hafez is a Fulbright Fellow, 2005, and a Rockefeller Fellow, 2009.

Nicola Trezzi (b. 1982, Italy) is an educator, exhibition maker, and writer based in Jaffa. From 2014 to 2017 he was the head of the MFA program at Bezalel Academy of Arts and Design Jerusalem and prior to this position he was U.S. Editor at *Flash Art International*. In February 2018, Trezzi will assume the post of director and chief curator of the CCA Tel Aviv.

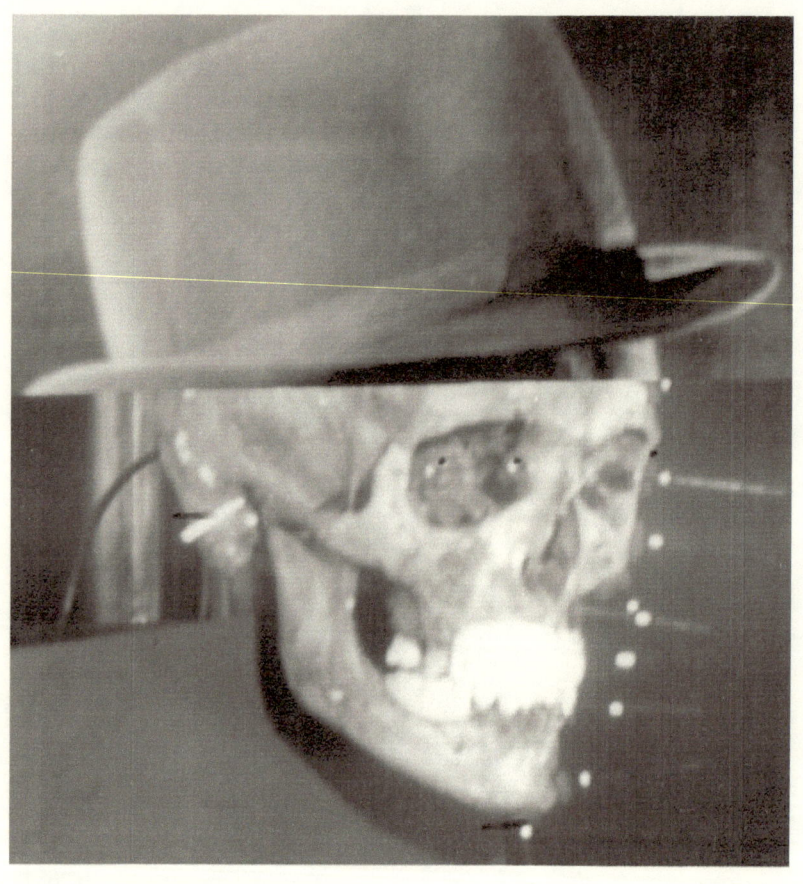

Mengele's Skull, 2012.
Thomas Keenan and Eyal Weizman

Prints on Acrylic, two video channels, 2:25, 2:36 mins.
Each 8 x 11 in. 20,5 x 28 cm.
Courtesy of the artists and Richard Helmer and Maja Helmer.

Mengele's Skull

by Thomas Keenan and Eyal Weiman

The installation *Mengele's Skull* documents the identification of the body of Auschwitz doctor Josef Mengele, exploring a forensic approach to evidence of war crimes. Mengele drowned in Brazil in 1979 and was exhumed in a suburb of São Paulo in 1985. Forensic scientist Richard Helmer superimposed Mengele's headshots and images of his skull with the help of novel video techniques. The ensuing identification process became a legal and technological turning point, relying on material evidence produced by scientific devices and experts, rather than the linguistic dimension of witness testimony.

Mengele's Skull examines the making of evidence through a historical forensic study. The scientific and technological analysis of photographic material documented in the installation eventually created highly aesthetic pictures. The work documents a methodological shift in the use of photography and other technologies for enhancing the image's evidentiary character as well as articulating a form of forensic aesthetics.

How To Make a Face Appear:
The Case of Mengele's Scull

by Heather Davis

It is now a trope of crime thrillers that the investigators spend as much time or more with the bones, DNA, hair, and other artifacts of the crime scene as they do with witnesses. Much of the drama takes place in labs, forensics departments, and other forums of scientific and medical investigation. In fact, witnesses are often proven to be unreliable, with fallible memories and sometimes falsified claims. Objects, on the other hand, are understood to unequivocally tell the truth of the matter. However, our understanding of this relation of evidence to truth did not always rely upon forensics. Rather, as Thomas Keenan and Eyal Weizman argue in their presentation of the case of *Mengele's Skull*, it was in 1985 that the object, in this case a skull, came to take on such deliberative weight.

Josef Mengele was the notorious Nazi who sadistically experimented with people in the name of eugenics. His crimes were so horrific that he was hunted until his death. Unfortunately, investigators arrived too late—six years after he drowned—and what followed was a transition in human rights law from the primacy of testimony to the language of the dead and their interpreters. In this transition, human rights law moved from listening to witnesses to reading marks on bones, from words to signs, from subjects to objects. As Keenan and Weizman write, "If the Eichmann trial marked, as Wieviorka claims, 'the advent of the witness,' then we will suggest here that the Mengele case constituted a parallel emergence of the 'thing.' But each of these processes did more than introduce new forms of evidence—they did nothing less than shift the conditions by which that evidence became audible and visible, the way juridical facts were constructed and understood."[1] What was being contested, beyond simply the facticity of Mengele's identity, was how we come to understand the world.

The appearance of Mengele after death in the haunting re-creation of his face overlaid on top of his skull, both represents the outcome and the evasion of justice. There is something satisfying in knowing that his body was unearthed from its burial place to be subjected to similar forms of scientific investigation that he cruelly and psychopathically inflicted on others. It is fitting for his bones to become an object of inquiry. And despite the fact that he was never forced to account for his deeds in life, what his exhumation did, besides confirming his identity, was provide a methodological practice for people seeking justice. For the same forensic practices that were honed in the process of his identification were then used to identify and put to rest the bodies of those who had been murdered by the state. In other words, the animation of Mengele's ghost was used to bring justice to those who suffered similar fates as his victims: "...it was the Mengele investigation that helped consolidate the interdisciplinary process for the identification of missing people, a set of techniques and operations which has since restored the names and identities of thousands of bodies."[2] By rendering Mengele an object of scientific knowledge, a kind of justice was forged through this new aesthetic language.

In the years since this investigation by Keenan and Weizman, the Forensic Architecture research team has developed a consulting agency for NGOs and an MA program, housed through the Centre for Research Architecture at Goldsmiths, University of London.[3] They have employed the techniques and practices of forensics to expand the understanding of what counts as evidence within international human rights law. They have documented and worked on numerous cases throughout the world that foreground not just the *figure*, the individual person, whether perpetrator or victim, but have worked to also show the ways in which the *field* has become the mechanism for genocide.[4] For example, in both the cases of *Guatemala: Operacion Sofia*[5] and *Ecocide in Indonesia*,[6] Forensic Architecture used satellite images and other mapping techniques to document how the governments of those countries have enacted genocide against indigenous peoples by literally removing the ground beneath their feet through deforestation and forced removal in Guatemala and the expansion of monocrops and fires in Indonesia. These practices result not just in the devastation of particular ecosystems, but ways of life, forms of human knowledge, and governance. Forensic aesthetics, and the artistic tools of visualizing these spatial practices, have fundamentally changed the nature of evidence once again, where the liveliness of things speaks volumes about the injustices of our world.

Notes:

1 Thomas Keenan and Eyal Weizman, Mengele's Skull: The Advent of a Forensic Aesthetics (Berlin: Sternberg Press, 2012), p 13.

2 Ibid, pp. 19-20.

3 The Centre for Research Architecture is a pedagogical experiment and political project that sits at the intersection of many fields and disciplines from architecture and media to law and climate science.

4 Eyal Weizman, "Introduction: Forensis," in Forensis: The Architecture of Public Truth, edited by Forensic Architecture (Berlin: Sternberg Press, 2014), pp. 9-32.

5 "Guatemala: Operacion Sofia" Environmental violence and genocide in the Ixil Triangle. 2009.

6 "Ecocide in Indonesia" Providing evidence to local and international bodies for universal jurisdiction cases in relation to environmental crime. 2015.

Thomas Keenan (b. 1959, U.S.) teaches media theory, literature, and human rights at Bard College, where he directs the Human Rights Project and helped create the first undergraduate degree program in human rights in the United States. He has served on the boards of a number of human rights organisations and journals, including *WITNESS, Scholars at Risk, The Crimes of War Project, The Journal of Human Rights*, and *Humanity*. He is the author of *Fables of Responsibility*, 1997; *Mengele's Skull*, with Eyal Weizman, 2012. He is co-editor, with Wendy Chun, *of New Media, Old Media*, 2006, 2nd ed. 2015; *of The Human Snapshot*, with Tirdad Zolghadr, 2013. *Flood of Rights*, co-edited with Suhail Malik and Tirdad Zolghadr, is forthcoming in 2016. He curated *Antiphotojournalism* with Carles Guerra, 2010-11 and *Aid and Abet,* 2011.

Eyal Weizman (b. 1970, Israel) is an architect, Professor of Spatial and Visual Cultures, and Director of the Centre for Research Architecture at Goldsmiths, University of London. Since 2011 Weizman directs the European Research Council funded project Forensic Architecture—on the place of architecture in international humanitarian law. He has worked with a variety of NGOs worldwide, and was a member of the B'Tselem board of directors. He lectured, curated, and organized conferences in many institutions worldwide. His books include *Forensic Architecture: Violence at the Threshold of Detectability*, 2017; *Mengele's Skull* with Thomas Keenan, 2012; *Forensic Architecture, dOCUMENTA 13 notebook*, 2012; *The Least of all Possible Evils*, 2009/2011; *Hollow Land*, Verso, 2007; *A Civilian Occupation*, 2003; the series *Territories* 1,2, and 3, *Yellow Rhythms* and many articles in journals, magazines and edited books.

Forensic Architecture is a research agency, based at Goldsmiths, University of London, that undertakes advanced architectural and media research on behalf of international prosecutors, human rights organizations, as well as political and environmental justice groups. As an emergent field, *Forensic Architecture* refers to the production and presentation of architectural evidence—buildings and larger environments and their media representations.

Heather Davis (b. 1979, Canada) is a researcher, writer, and editor from Montréal. Her current book project traces the ethology of plastic and its links to petrocapitalism. She explores and participates in expanded art practices that bring together researchers, activists, and community members to enact social change. She has written about the intersection of art, politics, ecology, and community engagement for numerous art and academic publications. She is the editor of *Art in the Anthropocene: Encounters Among Aesthetics, Politics, Environments and Epistemologies*, 2015, and *Desire Change: Contemporary Feminist Art in Canada*, 2017.

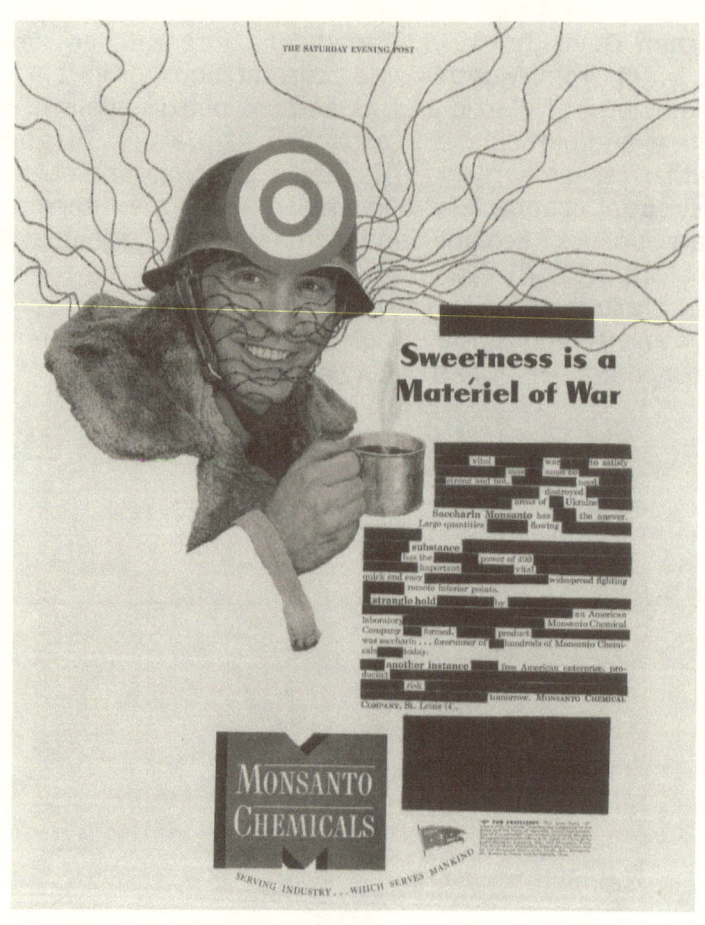

Sweetness is a Materiel of War, 2013
Kirsten Stolle

Collage, Monsanto magazine advertising,
colored paint chips, glitter, ink.
Each 11 x 8 ½ in. 28 x 22 cm.
Courtesy of the artist.

Monsanto Intervention

by Kirsten Stolle

Monsanto Intervention is a series of redacted and collaged Monsanto Chemical Company magazine advertisements from the 1940s to the 1960s, during which time the company promoted their chemicals for use in war, agriculture, and the home. By redacting, cutting, and drawing on the original text, the artist altered the intended messaging and reframed the visuals to expose the actual threats posed by the toxic chemicals being promoted. *52 New Chemicals* is derived from a 1947 *Fortune Magazine* advertisement for the Smith, Barney & Co. investment-banking firm's financial support of Monsanto; *Better Business*, also 1947, from an advertisement marketing insecticides for home, farm, and commercial applications; *Sweetness Is a Materiel of War*, from a 1947 *Saturday Evening Post* advertisement promoting saccharin to U.S. soldiers during sugar rationing in WWII; and *Shiner* from a 1942 *TIME* advertisement promoting the anti-corrosion compound Ferrisul, which was used in military weapons and particularly in targeting Hitler's regime.

Monsanto Intervention documents evidence of false advertising that led to environmental destruction. The display of misleading advertising can be legally prosecuted using scientific evidence of the toxicity of chemicals the advertisements promote. The work reflects the seductive visual language and textual rhetoric of printed advertisements for tracing the history of political and economic developments of highly problematic industries.

Chemical Interventions

by Mary Anne Redding

The late 1940s, 50s, and early 60s provide a post-atomic theater where artist Kirsten Stolle stages her interventions with near perfect hindsight. The post-world war period revealed new tensions between prosperous domestic contentment and the insidious menace of nuclear war. Unfortunately, the threat of one-upmanship on a nuclear platform is, again, an increasingly uncomfortable reality with volatile and narcissistic leaders like the newly inaugurated Donald J. Trump of America squaring off against North Korea's leader Kim Jong-un, tutored since birth in nefarious tactics by his no less disreputable father, Kim Jong-il.

During roughly the same time, Monsanto Chemical Company, originally formed in the US in 1901 and now a publically traded multinational agricultural biotech corporation, was aggressively marketing their chemical products through magazine advertisements. Although less publically, Monsanto was also heavily invested in pre-WWII activities researching uranium for use by scientists working to develop the first atomic bomb for the Manhattan Project. The 1930s saw Monsanto's first hybrid corn seed at the same time the company was expanding their research into new detergents, soaps, and industrial cleaning products, synthetic rubbers, and plastics.[1] Ubiquitous print propaganda promoted the company's chemicals for use in domestic contexts, agriculture and, of course, patriotic war efforts. Interestingly, but not surprisingly, Monsanto now bills itself as a "sustainable agricultural company" on its website and in present-day promotional material. Monsanto is currently the largest producer of genetically engineered (GE) seeds on the planet, accounting for almost one quarter (23%) of the global proprietary seed market and approximately ninety percent of GE seeds planted globally since 2003.[2]

What is important to understand is that, although difficult to comprehend from a 21st century perspective (that perfect hindsight again), in the 1940s and 50s, technology was seen as the ultimate answer and chemical advances were an important part of technology. Rapid developments in chemistry had stopped the Second World War and made America "safe" again, (sound familiar?). There was a pervading universal belief that went largely unchallenged: advances involving chemistry would unquestioningly make better lives. There was little awareness of the on-going collateral damage from using minimally, or worse, completely unregulated, chemicals. The concept that unseen, unsuspected chemical contaminants could cause harm over time was just beginning to seep around the edges of public consciousness.[3]

William Souder, in his 2012 biography about Rachel Carson, *On a Farther Shore*, credits her environmental classic, *Silent Spring*, published in 1962 with igniting the modern environmental movement. Trained as a zoologist and marine biologist, Carson worked as an editor and publicist for the U.S. Fish and Wildlife Service. Well aware of the global use of the pesticide DDT to fight malaria and other mosquito born illnesses on the battlefields and on civilians, Carson was part of the team at the Fish and Wildlife Service that began testing the harmful effects of DDT on fish and birds and its impact on the environment. These investigations were unprecedented; at that time, DDT was widely considered a "miracle chemical." In fact, the Nobel Prize in Physiology/Medicine 1948 was awarded to the Swiss industrial chemist, Paul Hermann Müller "for his discovery of the high efficiency of DDT as a contact poison against several arthropods."[4] Carson and her colleagues struggled with how to convince an unsuspecting public of the long-term effects of exposure to DDT when public health departments around the globe were staging safety demonstrations, newsreels touted its effectiveness, and international governments endorsed its usage.

Souder credits Carson with brilliantly linking the long-term use of DDT and other pesticides to the contamination of nuclear fallout—which terrified the public. The most controversial book of 1962/63 when Carson was appearing on television and testifying before Senate subcommittees about pesticides, *Silent Spring* revealed for the first time to a general readership: "the biological forces that link all life through the ages, the interdependence of living organisms and the continual cycling of nutrients and genetic material through species and over time."[5] Predictably, the major chemical companies fiercely opposed Carson's meticulous and irrefutable research, spending nearly a quarter of a million dollars to discredit the scientist. The editors at *Monsanto Magazine* tried to counter *Silent Spring* with their own essay, *The Desolate Year*, that graphically detailed how disease would spread and crops would fail without the use of pesticides. The terms of the environmental debate still raging today were established in the early 1960s: many scientists and environmentalist continue to challenge big business and government. The language established in the mid-century is nearly the same language used today when presenting arguments both supporting and denying scientific evidence in relation to climate change. In direct contrast to the events of 1962, when President John F. Kennedy commissioned a government investigation into the claims of *Silent Spring* that substantiated Caron's research, on January 20, 2017, the day Trump was inaugurated, the White House website was wiped clean of any references to climate change. This time it is the National Park Service, the Environmental Protection Agency, and their supporters that are carrying the torch for science in rogue or renegade twitter accounts that counter the apparent "gag orders" of the Trump administration.[6] Neither language nor politics have changed much in the last sixty some years except that information (real or fake) is spread much more rapidly thanks to ongoing advances in technology and the widespread use of the Internet.

How is evidence best presented or, in this case, re-presented? In her ongoing series *Monsanto Intervention*, Stolle alters and redacts mid-century Monsanto magazine advertisements pointing out a wrinkle in time. The Monsanto ads were ubiquitous, seen everywhere from *Life Magazine*, the *Saturday Evening Post*, *Fortune and Time* to many other popular magazines. Using primary and secondary source materials including 20th century medical books, agricultural magazines, archival photographs, U.S. Department of Agriculture promotional videos, and print advertisements, Stolle's work challenges the dominant public narrative, reflecting the artist's concern with industrial food production and the influence of biotechnology. Influenced by Carson and public radio, Stolle is firmly committed to the idea that art can bring new perspectives to contemporary scientific and social issues; through direct critique she challenges her audience to read between the lines. Using collage, cutting and drawing, Stolle redacts the original text of Monsanto's colorful publicity, altering the intended messaging and reframing the visuals to expose the true threat posed by toxic chemicals. The reconstructed ads criticize a history of overusing harmful agricultural chemicals and the U.S. government's weak regulations on corporate agribusiness. Her creative investigations continue to examine the influence of corporate agribusiness and biotech companies on the food supply. The artist asks us to consider the ongoing connection between influential corporate interests (read, financial bottom-line) and public health (read, a serious lack of information). Stolle's work focuses our attention on the motivations and deliberate misinformation propagated by the corporate machine.

Using public texts, Stolle creates elegant, carefully composed collages. Her layered, yet visually economical works probe issues of corporate green-washing, government propaganda, and agricultural rhetoric, exploring the complex relationships between economy and ecology, prompting the viewer to contemplate where their food comes from, how it was grown, and how the decisions big businesses make "behind the scenes" impact everyday choices about consumption. Stemming from personal health problems from eating GM soy products, Stolle became acutely aware of the potential risks of eating foods that contained genetically engineered ingredients. Since then, her artwork has been deeply grounded in a research-based practice making the personal political. An important note: neither Stolle nor Carson before her, were entirely against the use of chemicals altogether; rather, their argument is that the chemical industry with government support, was and is pushing the overuse of chemicals and genetically modified crops for economic gain at the expense of public health and the environment.

The titles Stolle uses in the *Monsanto Intervention* pieces are deliberately provocative, for example: *Sweetness is a Material of War*. How can war be sweet? What is marked out and why? What is the tension between what is seen and what is unseen? This viewer wants to scratch through the thick, deliberate black lines to reveal what has been covered. In the same way, we are asked to reread all paid advertising and ask is this claim true or is this false advertising? What is the hidden agenda here? Stolle's redacted text is hauntingly similar to many of the notorious and now public FBI files from the infamous McCarthy era of the 1950s, where thousands of Americans were accused of being communists or communist sympathizers—a charge leveled against Rachel Carson. McCarthyism refers to accusations of subversion or treason without evidence. Perhaps *Monsantoism* will have a similar connotation in the future, referring to the introduction of genetically modified substances to the food chain without sufficient testing as to their long-term effects. Stolle mimics the government's heavy-handed technique of blacking out words to obscure meaning, and in doing so, creates a kind of poetry, constructing truthful and relevant narrative.

In light of the current political upheaval in the United States and, indeed, the nationalistic tendencies around the world, Stolle's artwork takes on a greater importance as members of the U.S. government reject overwhelming scientific evidence of climate change. The Republican regime publically challenges the integrity of all journalists and the biases of the media, accusing them of propagating untruths—lies actually—in the face of empirical evidence. Art is, historically, one of the most potent antidotes to collective unconsciousness. Take Václav Havel's trajectory from philosopher/poet/playwright to political prisoner to the last president of Czechoslovakia/first president of the Czech Republic. Havel spent five years in and out of Communist prisons, lived for two decades under close secret-police surveillance and endured the suppression of his plays and essays. He served fourteen years as president, wrote nineteen plays, inspired a film, and a rap song and remained one of his generation's most seductively nonconformist writers.[7] Through all of the turmoil and considerable political and personal risk, Havel kept writing, kept agitating, kept faith in humanitarianism and environmentalism. Like Carson and Havel before her, Kirsten Stolle's artwork challenges us all to see the evidence in front of us even when it means sweeping out the propaganda to do so.

For Further Reading: Caron, Rachel with an introduction by Vice President Al Gore: *Silent Spring*. New York: Houghton Mifflin Company, 1994. Lear, Linda: Rachel Carson: *Witness for Nature*. New York: Henry Holt and Company, 1997. Souder, William: *On a Farther Shore: The Life and Legacy of Rachel Carson*. New York: Crown Publishers, 2012.

Notes:

1. Center for Global Research: The Complete History of Monsanto, "The World's Most Evil Corporation", September 15th, 2016 (last access February 2017).

2. GMWatch: The world's top 10 seed companies: who owns Nature, January 31, 2009 (last access February 2017) and MIT Mapping Controversies: Roundup Ready Crops – Cash crop or third world savior, Spring 2009 (last access February 2017).

3. KQED Forum with Michael Krasny. PBS Podcast (last access February 2017).

4. The Official Website of the Nobel Prize (last access February 2017).

5. Royte, Elizabeth: The Poisoned Earth: 'On a Farther Shore" by William Souder. The New York Times Sunday Book Review, September 14, 2012.

6. Davis, Wynne: It's Not Just the Park Service: 'Rogue' Federal Twitter Accounts Multiply, NPR. January 27, 2017.

7. Bilefsky, Dan and Jane Perlez: Václav Havel obituary, New York Times, December 18, 2011.

Kirsten Stolle (b. 1967, U.S.) is a visual artist working in collage, drawing, and site-responsive installations. Her research-based practice is grounded in the investigation of corporate propaganda, environmental politics and biotechnology. She appropriates practices of redaction, manipulation and distortion to confront industry misinformation. Her work examines the global influence of agrichemical and pharmaceutical corporations on our food supply and considers the connection between corporate interests and public health.

Her solo exhibitions include Turchin Center for the Visual Arts/ Appalachian State University, 2015; Dolby Chadwick Gallery 2010, 2007, 2005; ROY G BIV Gallery, 2016; and Kathryn Markel Fine Arts, 2002. Group exhibition include the San Jose Museum of Art 2016, 2013; Power Plant Gallery, Duke University, 2017; William King Museum, 2013; Monterey Museum of Art, 2005; Crocker Art Museum, 2004; Hunterdon Art Museum, 2006; Tweed Museum of Art, 2006; Riverside Art Museum 2005; Triton Museum of Art, 1995; University of North Carolina Asheville, 2012; Truman State University, 2014; Torpedo Factory, 2013; Roos Arts, 2013; Lesley Heller Workspace, 2016; and Jonathan Ferrara Gallery, 2013. Her work is included in the permanent collections of the San Jose Museum of Art; Crocker Art Museum and the Minneapolis Institute of Art.

Mary Anne Redding (b. 1960, U.S.) is a writer and curator. Currently she is the the curator and assistant director of the Turchin Center for the Visual Arts at Appalachian State University. She holds a B.A. in English Literature from Ohio University, an M.A. in Arts Administration from the School of the Art Institute of Chicago, an M.L.S. from the University of Illinois, Champaign Urbana, as well as an advanced certificate in Museum Studies from Arizona State University.

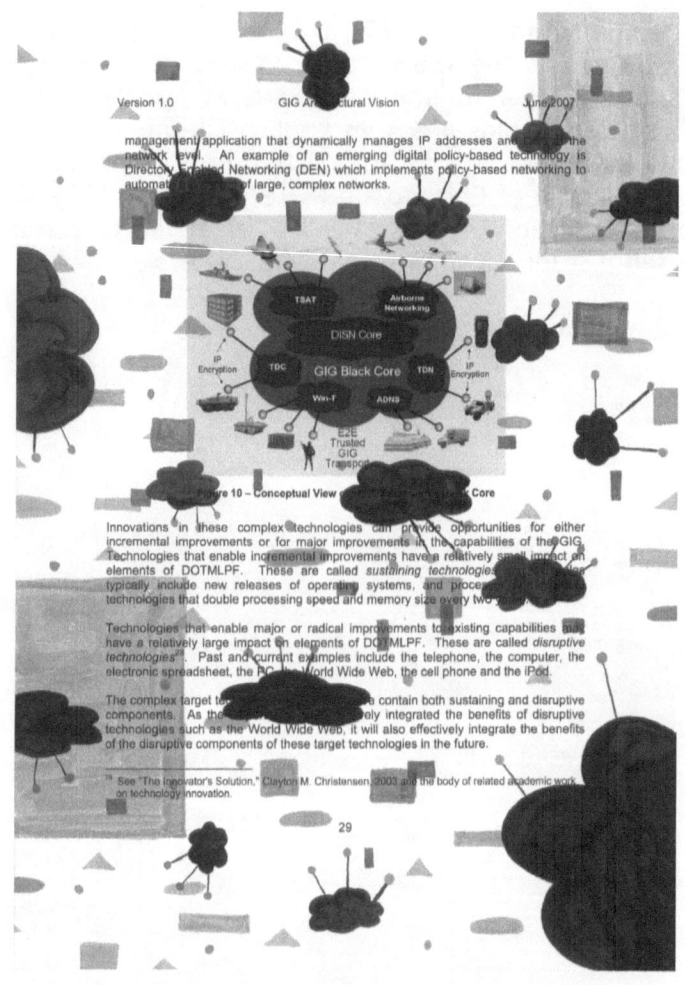

GIG-AV_V1_2007_P29, 2013.
Suzanne Treister

Inkjet and watercolor on Hahnemuhle Bamboo paper
Each 8 x 11 ½ in. 21 x 29,7 cm.
Courtesy of Annely Juda Fine Art, London and P.P.O.W., New York.

Camouflage

by Suzanne Treister

In the series *Camouflage*, watercolor is overlaid onto printed pages from documents downloaded from the Internet pertaining to U.S. Department of Defense programs such as the Global Information Grid. *Camouflage* was made in response to the public surprise at Snowden's revelations, many of which only confirmed what had already been reported by the U.S. press. The work's camouflaging of documentary information with watercolor thus perversely echoes back to this lack of public awareness.

Camouflage reveals evidence of state programs of mass surveillance. The watercolour patterns and drawings employ forms in the original documents to partially obscure and camouflage the evidence. The work visually discusses secrecy, disclosure, and circulation of classified information from intelligence agencies, using public and leaked documents as raw historical material for a visual representation of complex systems of state apparatuses.

Rendering The Evidence

by Giulia Bini

Being a machine is not a condition one can easily bear.

Suzanne Treister seems to embody the very nature of those mechanisms that are at the forefront of the debate concerning the breaking of global surveillance or financial rules, namely algorithms: a human in constant "high frequency," a sophisticated mind. She is able to deal with an incredible amount of data, at the same time transforming and mixing information with an apparently irrational drive.

In technocratic society, in reality, she's able to detect the pragmatic / operational structures through which systems and programmes of control perform their tasks and act on society, while at the same time researching the subterranean forces that accompany history in its unfolding.

Reflecting of the chameleonic and complex nature of the world, her artistic production covers a wide spectrum of disciplines, methods, systems of knowledge, and belief—ranging from cybernetics to the military and the scientific.

Her commitment to investigative practice has its roots in her biographical background. Of Polish-Jewish origin, Treister grew up in a family whose members had been persecuted, faced exile and concentration camps during World War II.

Her father's career, running a defense equipment spare-parts business, may also throw light upon her interest in researching the military.

Camouflage (2013) consists of selected pages from U.S. governmental documents overlapping with watercolour drawings.

The work is therefore situated at the intersection of the artist's investigative practice and her drawing/painting practice—a liminal position reflective of that of Treister herself.

Having worked on video games since the late 1980s, but uncomfortable with the post-modern atmosphere of the time, she felt a proximity to artists such as Mark Wallinger or Susan Hiller, who "wanted their work to investigate the world more directly."[1] At the same time, the need for a critical stance towards technology also led her to step back from media art, returning to other media such as drawing or painting.

The four works shown in the exhibition *Evidentiary Realism* are part of a series of thirty-four, presenting documents which the artist downloaded from the Internet, containing information on United States Department of Defense programs such as the Global Information Grid (GIG) and NetOps, and on which she superposed watercolours.

The GIG is an all-encompassing communications project enabling "the secure, agile, robust, dependable, interoperable data sharing environment for the Department where warfighter, business, and intelligence users share knowledge on a global network that facilitates information superiority, accelerates decision-making, effective operations, and Net-Centric transformation."[2]

The works on view in the exhibition are composed of documents dating from the period 2005-2008.[3]

The selected pages supply a lexicon of what can be considered an "organizational complex,"[4] illustrating the mechanisms of the contemporary controlled digital epoch:

Under the focus of the GIG Architectural Vision, are those technologies enabling Major and Radical Improvements to existing capabilities—so called disruptive technologies. UnderthefocusoftheNet—CentricEnvironmentwehave:Integration, efficiency, effectiveness of constructive interdependence achieved by moving from a platform to the Net—Centric environment. From the Department of Defense NetOps Strategic Vision (December 2008), the key words are: Superior decision making, shared understanding, agile force synchronization.[5]

Treister's attraction to evidence of global surveillance is not coincidental. Influenced by her father's "obsession with cross-referencing,"[6] in 2000 she worked on the website of his company, dealing with NATO materials, which were the origin of her mastering of military classification systems.

When Edward Snowden's files were revealed in 2013, Treister already had knowledge of the NSA project called Total Information Awareness (later renamed Terrorism Information Awareness) a programme dating back to 2003. Treister had worked on the former before Snowden's leak, which is why Snowden's data didn't constitute a surprise for her.

Camouflage proposes an active, constructive engagement with evidence, which goes beyond a binary understanding of it.

If on the one hand we have the "exposure" of evidence, on the second layer of the work, that of the drawings, what we find is what we could consider a rendering of evidence. While pointing to the camouflaged nature of the operation in question, the watercolour drawings also camouflage the evidence, paradoxically sabotaging its very function as proof.

Suzanne Treister notes: "By copying and repeating the motifs of the U.S. government documents in watercolour over each whole page I am in effect translating them into art, translating their meaning into a different register, that of art, and all its concomitant ramifications, from object of transcendence to market product."[7]

What the post-fact era requires is therefore an investigative practice, allowing the disclosure of organizational complexes that characterize the rise of technocracy, while at the same time dealing with the inner forces of control societies, thus revealing that "blurring of belief systems," which is precisely what Treister's vision and presentation of reality proposes. The basic actual facts testified by the documents-as-evidence, albeit camouflaged, remain operative, pragmatic, real.

The watercolours on the surface, portraying clouds with antennas, arrows and cones, patterns, planets and stars, are the ambivalent carriers of the art register, acting as alarms or alerts of the facts the artworks are evidence of.

Notes:

1. See Suzanne Treister's essay *From Fictional Videogame Stills to Time Travelling with Rosalind Brodsky 1991 – 2005*, 2004 (last access January 2017).

2. *NSA Documents Leaked by Anonymous*, June 7th, 2013 (last access January 2017).

3. For an example see: U.S. Department of Defense: Information Enterprise Architecture (DoD IEA) Version 2.0, July 2012 (last access January 2017). In terms of data gathering, there had been article in the Wall Street Journal in 2008 which clearly described the NSA's TIA programme and which Treister had exhibited at Raven Row in London in 2012 (last access January 2017).

4. The organizational complex" is defined as "architecture's immanence within a network of networks" or "the aesthetic and technological extension of what has been known since the early 1960s as the 'military-industrial complex'". Martin, Reinhold, *The Organizational Complex: Architecture, Media and Corporate Space*, Cambridge, MA: MIT Press, 2003, pp. 3-4.

5. *CAMOUFLAGE/ GIG-AV_V1_2007_P29 / Page 29 from the pdf: _7_GIG Architectural Vision – 200706v1.0.pdf (2007), CAMOUFLAGE/ N-CEJFC_V1_2005_P18 / Page 18 from the pdf: netcentric_jfc-1.pdf (2005), CAMOUFLAGE/ NetOpsSV_2008_P1. Page 1 from the pdf: DoD_NetOps_Strategic_Vision.pdf (2008); CAMOUFLAGE/ NetOpsSV_2008_P3_1. Page 3 from the pdf: DoD_NetOps_Strategic_Vision.pdf (2008), my emphasis.*

6. Cf. Luckhurst, Roger: *What Happens in the Gaps: An Interview with Suzanne Treister*, 2009 (last access January 2017).

7. Email conversation with the artist, 30.01.2017.

Suzanne Treister (b. 1958, UK) is a British artist. Initially recognized in the 1980s as a painter, she became a pioneer in the digital, new media, web based field from the beginning of the 1990s, making work about emerging technologies. Utilizing various media, including video, the Internet, interactive technologies, photography, drawing and watercolor, Treister has evolved a large body of work which engages with eccentric narratives and unconventional bodies of research to reveal structures that bind power, identity, and knowledge.

Her work has been shown at Bard Hessel Museum, New York, 2016; Liverpool Biennial, 2016; Muzeum Sztuki in Łódź, 2016-17; Bildmuseet, Umeå 2016-17; Victoria & Albert Museum, 2016; ICA, London, 1996 and 2015; Centre Pompidou, Paris, 2015; Kunstverein München, 2015; ZKM Center for Art and Media Karlsruhe, 2015; Stedelijk Museum Bureau, Amsterdam, 2015; Thyssen-Bornemisza Art Contemporary, Vienna, 2015; Hartware MedienKunstVerein, Dortmund, 2015; 10th Shanghai Biennale, 2014; 8th Montréal Biennale, 2014; Annely Juda Fine Art; P.P.O.W., 2013; Cleveland Institute of Art, 2013; Science Museum, London, 2006; Raven Row, London, 2012. Treister studied at St Martin's School of Art and Chelsea College of Art and Design, London.

Giulia Bini (b. 1984, Italy) is a curator and researcher working at the intersection between visual art, architecture and media. Her interests in media theory include the implications of an epistemological shift in science and technology, and its effects on interdisciplinary and emerging artistic practices.

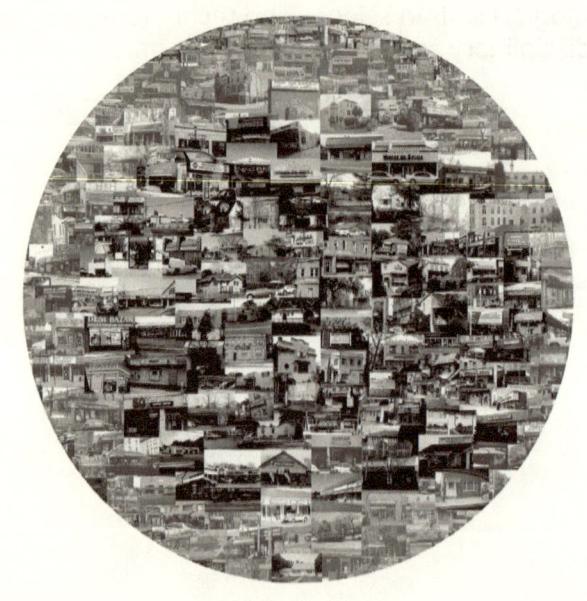

Information of Note, 2014.
Josh Begley

Composite image, C-Print.
40 x 40 in. 101,5 x 101,5 cm.
Courtesy of Robert Koch Gallery.

Information Of Note

by Josh Begley

Information of Note is composed of text and photographs extracted from the records of the NYPD Demographics Unit, which profiled Muslim-owned or affiliated businesses, gathering places, and sites of worship. Each entry includes a photograph of a venue's exterior, its name, address, and phone number, and the ethnicity of the owners. Many of the observations are quite banal—together they paint an unremarkable portrait of quotidian life. The NYPD Demographics Unit program "never generated a lead," according to the Associated Press. These surveillance programs were secret until a large number of internal NYPD documents were leaked to the press in 2011.

Information of Note presents evidence of secret surveillance programs marked by social bias and racial profiling. The work explores the gathering of information by state power structures and those who scrutinize them. The evidentiary dataset has a nonlinear form, taking shape from metadata, searches, and indexing. Combining the photographic medium with processing data, the work composes a collage reminiscent of surveillance software interfaces.

The Eye Of The Law

by Nijah Cunningham

We said it before and it has to be said again: the law is not justice.[1] This is a simple enough proposition. But the measure between life and death tends to fall on this distinction between the law in its many manifestations (e.g. the judge, the district attorney, the police, and the gun) and the call for justice. Josh Begley is aware of this distinction and uses his artistic practice to explore the limits of the legal system we live under and an elusive justice that is yet to come.

Begley makes data visualizations. He scrapes information off the web and creates visual interventions that blur the boundary between the seen and unseen. But Begley's visualizations do even more. They expose the law's impotence and unreason. It is only after realizing the law's powerlessness that we become aware of the viscous means through which it seeks out its own self-preservation. Begley's projects add to the remarkable work of visual artists who explore the moral-political dimensions of visibility and expose the complex systems that both govern the limits of the intelligible and maintain the parameters of possible claims of injury and redress. Yet, Begley is more preoccupied with the law's construction of vision. He forces us to bear witness to the abstract operations that undergird the law's claim to the capacity of sight. The question for Begley is no longer primarily a question about old and new visibilities, such as surveillance, but, instead, it is a question about the complex set of practices, relations, images, and imaginaries that that constitute the legal system's faculty of seeing. This is the object of Begley's concern and the source of what we might describe as a kind of realism. He is ultimately concerned with how the law's sight becomes an evident and unquestionable fact. He forces us to slow down and ask how the law gained its capacity to see and contend with the operations that constitute that act of seeing.

Realism is just another word for describing how Begley's visualizations distill and break open the component parts of images, data, and other forms of visibility. He tells us, "just as the best novels don't have a singular point, some visualizations live in a space, a terrain. They are traversing the landscape of a question, trying to catch a glimpse of some fleeting thing."[2] For Begley, visualizations disrupt the normative logics of representation. To be sure, when he refers to the "best novels" Begley has Toni Morrison in mind. More specifically, he is thinking about the sensibility that animates her narratives as they strain the equivalence of time and history; reorder the past, present, and future shuttle between different points of view; and refuse closure. It can be said that Begley learned the art of visualization by thinking with Morrison. In *Subject of the Dream*, Begley moves from the page to the screen as he cuts and pastes different excerpts from Morrison's novels to create a collage. He breaks apart and reassembles the text in order to conjure a subplot from the interstices of Morrison's works. When we read Begley's text, we discover the kind of polyvocality, shifting perspectives, fragmentary narrative, play of absence and presence, and refusal of closure that we find in Morrison's writing. Morrison's aesthetic sensibility inspires Begley's testing of the visual interface of phones and computer screens and his experimentation with the long-scroll. Do we experience a story differently if there are no pages to turn? When we notice the different tones of the pages he pastes together are we made more or less aware of the original sources these excerpts came from? How does the collage transform our experience of the screen? Does the scroll extend the story or do we, with each scrolling gesture, stir up traces of the absent texts that make the story possible? Do we read the words strung together or are we meant to watch the variations of beige, grey, peach, and blue as they shift across the screen like reminders of the negative space that each excerpt has left behind? All of these questions emerge out the visual encounter that Begley creates in *Subject of the Dream* as he injects absence and uncertainty into a medium that is usually charged with a promise of verisimilitude. As the corny adage goes: seeing is believing. But belief is not only a question of what or why but also *how*. It is through reading Morrison that Begley learns the significance of composition in his works; how, instead of simply showing or explaining given facts, visualizations must interrogate the ways things come together. Good visualizations, like good novels, bring into sharp focus the fissures, breaks, and omissions that make any given story tellable. This, to my mind, is what it means to "travers[e] the landscape of a question." And, if anything, what we encounter in *Subject of the Dream* is Begley's first steps in the direction of a question that would eventually lead him to interrogate seeing as a self-legitimizing operation of the law.

The law is powerless when confronted by the call for justice. And it is precisely when an injustice reveals its mythical foundations that the legal system starts seeing things, starts looking for what can be made into evidence.

The photographs that make up *Information of Note* were among the documents from the New York Police Departments Demographics Unit leaked in 2011 that exposed a secret surveillance program that monitored American Muslims across New York City for almost a decade. Notice how Begley arranges the photographs. Placed side-by-side, the cars, storefront signs, awnings, and trees that cut across each photograph produce a mosaic-effect. There is nothing "panoptic" here. The mundane snapshots fail to cohere into a totalizing image. We do not see the target population of this program. In fact, the composition of *Information of Note* makes it difficult to apprehend what is captured inside the frame of each photograph. We have to come in close and almost press our faces on the work to notice where one photograph ends and the other begins. Ultimately, we encounter an accumulation of spaces in this work. Sidewalks, street corners, storefronts, front yards, driveways, and parking lots are all condensed into a circle. From afar, we notice placement of the color photographs vis-à-vis the black-and-white photographs. We see the faint outlines of concentric circles. An outer ring of color surrounds the black-and-white in the center, rendering *Information of Note* into a kind of mosaic of an iris and a dilated pupil. In this way, Begley assembles the photographs of NYPD's secret surveillance program into a depiction of the *eye of the law*.

Information of Note is a brilliant response to the comments made by Chief Thomas Galati of the NYPD's Intelligence Bureau in his deposition as part of the civil rights brought against the New York Police Department following the 2011 leak. In order to justify the surveillance program, despite the fact that none of the materials collected provided any leads, Galati gives a quick reading of one of the Departments Demographics Unit's reports: "I'm seeing Urdu. I'm seeing [the police officers] identify the individuals involved in that are Pakistani [...] I'm using that information for me to determine that this would be a kind of place that a terrorist would be comfortable in."[3] The eye of law transforms spaces into places of potential unlawful activity. Here, sight is mobilized to preserve the authority of the legal system and justify the secret surveillance program. Galati's claim to this curious form of sight should not be confused with the act of reading.[4] Rather, "seeing Urdu" sets into motion a complex operation in which the recognition of a spoken language transforms a space into a "kind of place that a terrorist would be comfortable in." Elsewhere, Galati elaborates on this synesthetic process of transformation:

The language spoken at a location is a piece of information which can be useful should the NYPD be pursuing a terrorist, conducting an investigation, or trying to gather information about potential unlawful activity due to events occurring domestically or abroad. Among other things, under exigent circumstances, a unique language environment can help law enforcement officers choose which locations to visit first when search for an unidentified individual who has been reported.[5]

Information of Note demonstrates how the *eye of the law* creates these "language environments." In Begley's visualization, we see how Galati's claim of seeing Urdu weaves the photographs together. Where we see a collection of mundane snapshots of random spaces the *eye of the law* sees a series of locations of concern. Begley demonstrates how the *eye of the law* "sees" by going beyond seeing in the service of justifying the law's unlawful activity.

The *eye of the law* does not see a thing. Its purpose is to conjure things from the dark and produce evidence where there is none in the service of concealing what the law already knows about itself.

Notes:

1. See Nijah Cunningham and Tiana Reid, *Blue Life*, *The New Inquiry*, August 10, 2017

2. Josh Begley, *Setting Tangents Around a Circle*, presented at Eyeo Festival, Walker Art Center, Minneapolis, Minnesota, June 8, 2016.

3. Thomas Galati qtd. in Adam Goldman and Matt Apuzzo, *NYPD: Muslim spying led to no leads, terror cases*, Associated Press, August 21, 2012 (accessed November 8, 2017).

4. My thanks to Daniela Gandorfer for her insight, advice, and her call for us to "rethink out modes of reading law" which have aided me in this engagement with Begley's work. See Daniela Gandorfer, "Deleuze and Guattari's *A Thousand Plateaus*, Law, and Synesthesia," Nietzsche 13/13, November 5, 2016 (accessed November 8, 2017).

5. United States District Court Southern District of New York, Declaration of Thomas Galati, Handschu v. Special Services Division 71, Civ. 2203 (CSH).

Josh Begley (b. 1984, U.S.) is a data artist and developer. Appropriating publicly available satellite imagery, Begley's work takes advantage of application programming interfaces, or APIs, to build collections of machine-generated images about quotidian life. He currently works at *The Intercept* with the journalists Jeremy Scahill, Glenn Greenwald, and Laura Poitras. His work has appeared in *The New York Times*, *The Atlantic,* and *Wired*, among others. Begley holds degrees from the University of California, Berkeley and New York University.

His work has been included in shows at major institutions and galleries, such as: *Laura Poitras: Astro Noise*, Whitney Museum of American Art, New York, 2016; *Watching You, Watching Me*, Open Society Foundations, Budapest, Hungary, 2015; *The Crypto Design Exhibition*, Museum of The Image, Breda, Netherlands, 2015; *Necessary Force*, University of New Mexico, Albuquerque, 2015; *Prison Obscura*, The New School, New York, 2015; *Web on the Wall*, Robert Koch Gallery, San Francisco, 2014; *Moving Walls 22*, Open Society Foundations, New York, 2014; *Prison Obscura*, Cantor Fitzgerald Gallery, Haverford, 2014; Art Dubai, Global Art Forum, Dubai, United Arab Emirates, 2013; Adhocracy, New Museum of Contemporary Art, New York, 2013.

Nijah Cunningham (b.1985, U.S.) specializes in African American and African diasporic literature and his fields of interest include black studies, performance studies, visual culture, gender and sexuality, and postcolonial criticism. Titled Quiet Dawn: Time, Aesthetics, and the Afterlives of Black Radicalism, his current book project reconsiders the material legacies of the revolutionary past by exploring questions of embodied performance, temporality, and the archive as they relate to the 1960s. Ultimately, this project attends to modes of experience and practice that fall outside of normative accounts of black radical politics but, nonetheless, gesture to worlds that could have been. He is currently a fellow at Princeton University. He is currently a Cotsen fellow at the Princeton Society of Fellows.

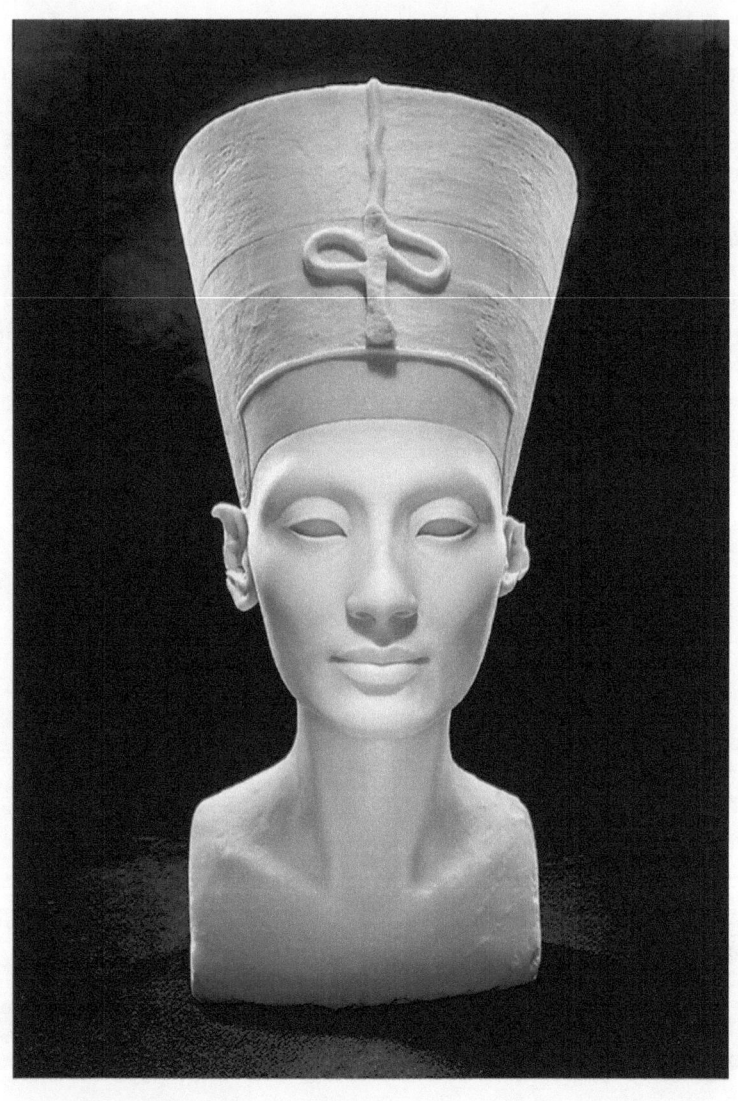

The Other Nefertiti, 2015.
Nora Al-Badri & Jan Nikolai Nelles

3D print polymer resin.
20 x 13 x 9 ½ in. 50 x 33 x 24 cm.
Courtesy of the artists and NOME Gallery.

The Other Nefertiti

by Nora Al-Badri and Jan Nikolai Nelles

The Other Nefertiti is a 3D-printed replica of the Nefertiti Bust, an ancient Egyptian artifact housed in the Neues Museum in Berlin. The artwork's creation entailed the release of a high-resolution 3D data file that was shared freely on the Internet. The work stands as proof of colonial pillaging and challenges notions of national ownership; it considers the role of copying in preservation and access to evidence in relation to global heritage. The project received wide media coverage for its unauthorized 3D scan of the artifact inside the museum and its public release despite the copyright holder's exclusive reproduction rights.

The Other Nefertiti embodies archeological evidence and its history of ownership throughout civilizations. The copying of artifacts in physical and digital forms points to the ever-improving technical reproduction of evidence and ways in which authenticity can be discussed openly in online forums, while the sharing and collaborative preservation avoid restrictions and suppression of evidence. The artwork combines the politics and the aura of an unique historic artifact in the age of its reproducibility.

Conflicting Evidence

by Susanne Leeb

To correct the unintentional error committed in 1913, the Berlin Museum declares itself ready and willing to return the head of the queen, the object of disagreement, to the Cairo Museum.[1]

This memorandum was written by Egyptologist Pierre Lacau in 1931; commissioned by the French government, Lacau served as director of the Department of Antiquities in Cairo from 1914 to 1936. Due to Adolf Hitler's veto in 1933, the agreed upon return never took place. Since then, Nefertiti has been in Berlin. With their "other Nefertitis," the artists Nora Al-Badri and Jan Nikolai Nelles intervene in this field, still very controversial today: that of colonial excavations around the year 1900, and thus questions of ownership, the production of "cultural goods," and the value of collector's items.

The Source of the Conflict

Evidentia is a figure of accumulation in rhetoric. A main thought is divided into parts that explain the main idea in variations to make it seem obvious. Evidence is created from a chain of arguments, or from a variation of the main idea. In the case of the question of where the Nefertiti bust belongs, still controversial today, there are two conflicting main thoughts: for Western museums, it is evident that they have the right to possess the cultural heritage of other countries. For critics of this argument, it is evident that they have no such right. At issue is not the renationalization of culture or the question of an authentic context, but the conditions of injustice during colonialism under which the objects first came to Europe or to other Western collections where they are now considered invaluable treasures.

Nefertiti 1.0

Museums create their evidence in various ways: juridically, aesthetically, academically, architecturally. The staging of Nefertiti within a museum temple in a glass case, standing on its own, the only piece in a dark hall, makes it into an absolute "highlight" of the collection. This framing is a "partial thought" that serves to make the main thought seem evident. "Nefertiti is the most beautiful woman in Berlin," as has been said ever since the 1920s, and she belongs here. But this includes an entire apparatus of scholarship and narratives according to which these objects would no longer exist without Western archaeological research or that they would have been destroyed in the countries where they were found.[2] In the case of Nefertiti, in turn, it is also argued that there has been no official demand for restitution on the part of the Egyptian government. The demands of various antiquities authorities have always been dismissed by saying that they were issued by the "wrong" authority. For example, although Zahi Hawass, the former Egyptian Minister of State for Antiquities Affairs and previously the Secretary General of the Egyptian Supreme Council of Antiquities, had been trying to regain the statue since 2002, he was at this point in his career not part of the government itself, even if he later became part of it briefly. In the case of archaeological artifacts, museums refer primarily to the legality of the division of archaeological finds. In certain regions, the division of finds only took place in the mid-1920s or later, so that a great many artifacts had already left the country before such agreements. In addition, the division of finds under colonialism did not necessarily involve sharing the finds with the colonized region, but first and foremost with the respective colonial power. In the case of Egypt, the situation was even more complicated: the colony was under British rule, but the French were those responsible for archaeological sites and finds. German archaeologists and the French agreed on dividing up the finds, but the conditions under which Nefertiti could be removed from the country without expert evaluation on site give cause for speculation about the possible illegality of the transport.[3]

For Bénédicte Savoy, who recently reconstructed this history, the sharing of the finds that took place on January 20, 1913 was "the result of an administrative, diplomatic, and personal constellation in which French-British rivalries played as great a role as the policy practiced for decades by the French antiquities administration policy of laissez faire regarding foreign excavators."[4] Symptomatically, Egypt has no place in this conflict of rivalries: it was not a sovereign state, but a British colony. The legality of the possession thus seems evident, since an argument to keep the bust where it is remains in the framework of the narration that made the objects what they are: finds from the colonial period, objects of scholarly research, and ancient "treasures" and legally valid because the laws either of the colonial powers or the nation-state that insists on protecting the property of their own holdings. But this very evidence is controversial, for not a single partial thought takes the Egyptian perspective. For others, it is much more evident that Nefertiti belongs in Egypt. And this applies not just to the Egyptian Ministry of State for Antiquities. If you ask people in Egypt about the statue, few are aware that it is not located in an Egyptian museum. As a copy, the image of Nefertiti is omnipresent in Egypt. If you say that it is located in a German museum, the most common, usually indignant answer is that it's not right, that she belongs to Egypt. Beside this subjective sense of injustice or the discussion of cultural identity, relations of power and inequality relations are inscribed in the "acquisition" or the "collection" of these cultural goods. With the frequent recourse to legality as a form of justification, no mention is made of the context of colonial politics, although archeology has for some time now engaged in self-critique about its involvement in colonialism.[5] Although the division of finds was legal according to the understanding at the time, the ethical framework and archeology's own self-conception have changed dramatically.

Nefertiti 2.0

Since a political decision is not in sight at the moment—and in light of the fact that Western collections make up a large part of Africa's cultural heritage, the question cannot be clarified just in terms of Nefertiti—artists and cultural workers have the opportunity to intervene in the discourses, forms of value production, public opinion formation, a discussion on the ethics of collecting and in the power relations of knowledge production. *The Other Nefertiti* is accordingly more than a true-to-original 3D print of the bust. It also includes a video that acts out an excavation find, a video that shows the scanning process in the museum, the open source publication of the print data and finally discursive formats—a podium discussion in Cairo on the question of the relationship between contemporary art and heritage, hosted by the artists in Cairo together with the Goethe-Institut.[6] In the age of the post-factual, the art of falsification needs to be defended, because in art artifice is not used to conceal a truth or to spread an untruth but to address a problem. This problem becomes visible in disclaimers or in the transparency of the construction. In this sense, Nora Al-Badri and Jan Nikolai Nelles have created an excavation video filmed on the Egyptian coast where a second Nefertiti bust is found. In the age of the digital, the reference no longer guarantees the authenticity of what is presented, but conventionalized framing conditions serve as a warranty: the form of recording—shaky, grainy, poor quality—the time code in the shot, the plausibility of the situation in which a film was recorded, and not least the site of circulation, that is, the platforms in which a video is made public. Secret, illicit excavations take place on a nightly basis in Egypt. The find is usually documented by videos made using bad cameras shot by flashlight. These find-videos are then uploaded onto certain platforms to sell the pieces on the black market. Such framing conditions are easily imitated, and in this way the "fact" is created that a second Nefertiti was found. By raising the question of where the original Nefertiti is, the focus is placed not only on the current place of custody and the question of possession, but also on the black market, where all forms of collecting antiquities are ultimately involved. If the objects at the time were purchased for a ridiculously low price or simply distributed in the framework of dividing up the finds, now the objects are worth millions. But this contributes to the emergence of the black market that Al Badri/Nelles bring attention to in their video. One of the participants in the Cairo podium discussion Monica Hanna, a member of the Egyptian archaeological NGO the Egypt Heritage Task Force, also reported of the "underside" of archaeological knowledge. On Facebook, the EHTF documents illicit excavations, illegal sales, or neglect of cultural heritage sites by the Egyptian government. A secondary effect of ownership is the copyright on replicas or images of the original that "belongs" to an institution. The release of 3D print data as open-source makes it possible for many people to create an exact replica of the Nefertiti statue. Since Nelles and Al-Badri's public release of the data in December 2015, the artists have received numerous requests from universities (some from Egypt itself) whether the data could be used for academic purposes or they were asked if the data was available for commercial use. Since then, thousands of 3D prints and digital remixes have been made all over the world and posted online. The digital replication of the bust has opened a new digital space, independent of the institutions. This form of participation was a central idea behind the artists' action. Even if the print out in its original size in good quality is relatively expensive—a high quality 3D print costs currently 6000 euros—it can also be made in poorer quality for 100 euros—the data allows for the possibility of reproduction without permission of the museum and the fees related to this. In the wake of the data's release, the museums have declined to take any legal action. But the original is impossible to separate from its reproductions. The ubiquitous presence of the copies will not solve the problem linked to the ownership of the original. The Berlin Nefertiti continues to provide the gold standard for all reproductions.

Even if Al-Badri and Nelles concretely intervene in one of the secondary effects of possession, their work poses the greater question of who owns what works and why in what value systems the notion of original and copy circulate. The artists simply demand what the museums claim to be: world heritage that all have access to. With *The Other Nefertiti*, they also show to what extent museums have distanced themselves from their own declared self-understanding.

Note:

1. Cairo, July 1, 1931, memorandum written by Pierre Lacau on the bust of Nefertiti.

2. There is now an entire sub-branch of archaeology involved in critiques of these narratives in the form of an intellectual history of the discipline. See for example Lynn Meskell, ed., Archaeology Under Fire: Nationalism, Politics and Heritage in the Eastern Mediterranean and Middle East (London: Routledge 1998); Colin Renfrew, Loot, Legitimacy and Ownership: The Ethical Crisis in Archaeology (London: Duckworth, 2000); Zainab Bahrani, Zeynep Çelik, and Edhem Eldem, eds., Scramble for the Past: A Story of Archaeology in the Ottoman Empire 1753-1914 (Istanbul: SALT, 2011).

3. For a reconstruction of the early history of the Nefertiti find with references to other literature, see Bénédicte Savoy, ed., Nofretete. Eine deutsch-französische Affäre 1912-1931 (Cologne: Böhlau, 2012).

4. Ibid., 12.

5. Oscar Moro-Abadía, "The History of Archaeology as 'Colonial Dicourse,'" in: Bulletin of the History of Archaeology 16 (2), 8 (last accessed on Feb, 4, 2017). Oscar Moro-Abadia sums up the most important aspects: archaeologists contributed to a colonial discourse in the form of knowledge of power over the past. They created a romantic image of archaeological practice that in the 19th century was linked to a focus on spectacular discoveries of "lost civilizations." They omitted the link between colonial expansion and a field of scholarship and justified the appropriation of material cultures from the colonized regions.

6. See The Actuality of the Ancient: Contemporary Art, Icons and Identity November 30, 2015 (last accessed on March 1, 2017).

Since 2009 **Nora Al-Badri and Jan Nikolai Nelles** have been working together as a collective, based in Berlin. Their works interfere in social infrastructures through controversial performances that challenge institutions. The collective pursues a critical re-evaluation of actual cultural commons, the power of representation through material objects of other cultures, their digital image as well as the concepts of heritage and identity politics.

Their works have been on display in various exhibitions and institutions such as the 4th Thessaloniki Biennale of Contemporary Art, 2013; the Victoria & Albert Museum, Applied Arts Pavilion at La Biennale di Venezia, 2016; and the 3rd Design Biennial, curated by Anselm Franke, Istanbul, 2016. Their works got granted by several institutions like Haus der Kulturen der Welt (HKW), Goethe-Institut, Institut für Auslandsbeziehungen (IfA), the German Federal Foreign Office and the European Cultural Foundation (ECF).

Nora Al-Badri (b. 1984, Germany) is a multi-disciplinary artist with a German-Iraqi background. Her practice incorporates interventions and different mediums such as sculpture and installation, photography and film. She studied political sciences at Johann Wolfgang Goethe University in Frankfurt/Main and visual communications at Offenbach University of Art and Design.

Jan Nikolai Nelles (b. 1980, Germany) is a multi-disciplinary artist. His artistic practice oscillates between different fields such as visual and media art, documentary filmmaking, and cultural activism. He graduated from Offenbach University of Art and Design in 2011. In the past, he founded an independent project space in Frankfurt/Main, Germany, and co-founded a photography magazine.

Susanne Leeb (b. 1968, Germany) is an art historian and critic. She graduated in art history, philosophy, German literary studies at the University of Cologne. For three years she worked as co-editor of Texte zur Kunst, the leading magazine for contemporary art and art theory in Germany. In 2007 she took her doctoral degree from the Europa-Universität Viadrina in Frankurt/Oder with a dissertation on The Art of the Others. Worldart and the Anthropological Configuration of Modernity. Since 2007 Susanne Leeb has been research associate at the collaborative research center Aesthetic Experience at the Freie Universität Berlin. After an assistant-professorship in Basel, she has been since 2014 Professor for contemporary art at the Institute for Philosophy and Art History (IPK) at the Leuphana Universität Lüneburg.

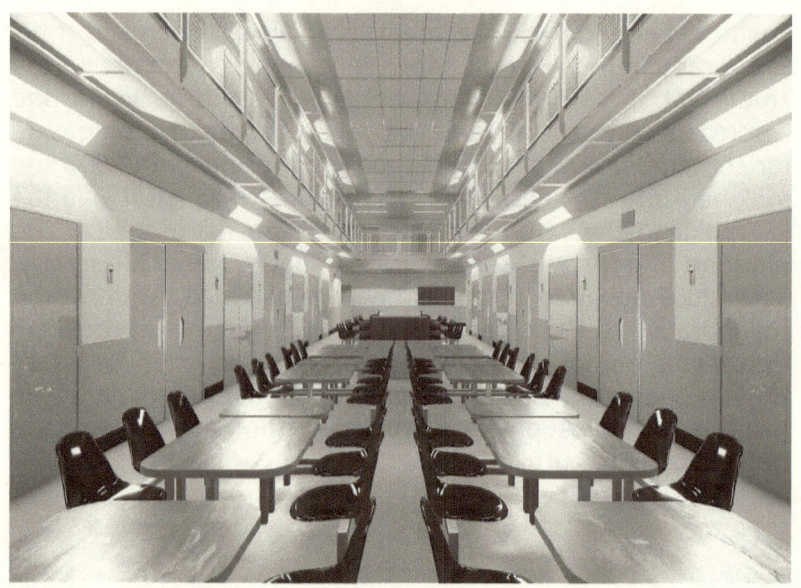

Seamless Transitions, 2015.
James Bridle

Digital video projection,
one channel, 5:28 min.
1920 x 1708 px.

Seamless Transitions was commissioned by The Photographers' Gallery, London, and supported by Nome, Berlin. Public funding by the National Lottery through Arts Council England.
Animation by Picture Plane.

Seamless Transitions

by James Bridle

Seamless Transitions is a 3D video tour of three British sites of immigration detention, trial, and deportation: Field House, home of the Special Immigration Appeals Commission (SIAC), designed for the presentation of secret evidence; Harmondsworth IRC at Heathrow, part of the UK's detention estate; and the Inflite Jet Centre. Modeled on planning documents and eyewitness accounts, the work re-creates these highly political but architecturally bland spaces that denied asylum seekers pass through before their rendition by air—spaces that are otherwise invisible in public life.

Seamless Transitions unveils the secret infrastructure of detention, judgment, and deportation. It applies a forensic sensibility to 3D demonstrative evidence for visualizing the architecture, administration, and politics of high-security sites. Proceeding from the history of visual perspective and the representation of complex spatial and social systems, these investigative strategies for capturing and rendering reality with 3D reconstructions have the potential to expand the field of visibility and public accountability.

Infrastructural Violence:
The Smooth Spaces Of Terror

by Susan Schuppli

As tracking shots and image pans move us through a sequence of locations enveloped in the computational veneer of synthetic architecture, the cinematic capture of corporate culture merges with the super-mesh of carceral space. A high resolution labyrinth of empty corridors, closed doors, waiting rooms, and seating areas that "transitions seamlessly" into security fences, gated zones, and a secret court. The steady illumination of these interior spaces defies their temporal specificity as day becomes continuous with night. But this brightness too will soon morph into the black-hole darkness of a covert operation as we exit onto airport tarmac where a private jet awaits, its stairway extended and cabin door agape.

There is something deeply sinister in the relentless perfection of these multiplying screen spaces emptied of human presence. Dread streams from their plasmatic pixels and violence lurks beneath their digital cladding. These are the unseen spaces of British law and order where decisions as to immigration and practices of deportation take place: Harmondsworth Immigration Removal Centre near Heathrow; the Special Immigration Appeals Court in the City of London with its architectural provisions for the presentation of evidence in secret; and the Inflite Jet Centre at Stansted Airport, a private terminal re-purposed after hours by the Home Office to deport migrants whose asylum claims have been rejected or whose biographies link-up with locations suspected of anti-western sympathies.

Through a combination of investigative strategies and 3D computer modelling, artist James Bridle takes us into sites that are off-limits to cameras and recording technologies or to those without proper security clearance. Spaces where detainees wait out their days in crowded conditions without access to proper legal advice and healthcare, where the accused and their lawyers are denied from seeing the documents that set out the grounds for their deportation, or where private tour buses arrive in the middle of the night. Even the executive lounge in the airport terminal at Stansted withdraws from the regime of visibility when its human cargo switches from its elite business clientele to that of the dispossessed. Despite the proximity of these sites to many million inhabitants in the UK, knowledge of their presence and the activities that take place within is very limited and expressly designed to restrict them from public scrutiny. Criticism of the security practices that have emerged as part of Britain's expanding arsenal of anti-terror legislation is mitigated when civic engagement is diminished. As Bridle makes clear in his writing and commentary, reducing the field of visibility reduces demands for greater public accountability.[1]

These clandestine architectures and the logistical networks in which they operate are key components in what I call the "infrastructural violence" of the global war on terror that results in the systematic erosion of rights as well as the legal guarantees of citizenship. Yet Bridle, in visualising Britain's hidden spaces of detention and deportation, does more than simply bring the unseen into public view and therefore into public discourse. With the use of video wall technology and CGI he also makes explicit the degree to which the smooth surfaces of data-space will produce the very screens on which the war on terror and its various protagonists will wage their battles —their de facto image wars—from the televisual interface of armed drone surveillance and combat, to the online release of Islamic State videos.

Indeed as I write this text, I cannot help but reflect upon Article 13 of the Geneva Convention, which states "prisoners of war must at all times be protected, particularly against acts of violence or intimidation and against insults and public curiosity." This is the Article that prohibits States from trafficking in images of prisoners that can be used for propagandistic purposes or could exploit their misery for salacious reasons such as selling newspapers, although the Article's legal interpretation has been widely disputed as to who and what technically constitutes a State actor. For example, Al Jazeera's decision to release photos of U.S. soldiers killed in Iraq in 2003 prior to their families being informed was hugely controversial, whereas the publication of images of Guantanamo Bay inmates by the U.S. was deemed permissible and even in the interests of national security, because the prisoners' legal classification as "illegal enemy combatants" didn't offer them the same protection accorded to prisoners of war.[2]

With the 2014 killing of British aid worker Alan Henning, the government even went so far as to suggest that the very act of watching the Islamic State execution video could be deemed a criminal act punishable under law. On October 5th *The Independent* ran a cover with a black square designating an unimaginable image with the caption "On Friday a decent, caring human being was murdered in cold blood. Our thoughts are with his family. He was killed, on camera, for the sole purpose of propaganda. Here is the news, not the propaganda."

In attributing extraordinary moral powers of persuasion to images, Article 13 confirms the consequential nature of images as potential instruments of political violence such that their production and circulation must be closely monitored by the State. On the one hand we have a Convention that set out to protect the human dignity and rights of subjects incarcerated by the State during times of conflict and war by limiting the circulation of their photographs. And on the other (the sites presented in *Seamless Transitions*) there is deliberate obfuscation of the very images that would ultimately help to hold the State accountable for potential human rights violations, by shedding light on practices that take place under the cover of a virtual image-ban. Certain kinds of images are considered so morally reprehensible that they must be barred or withdrawn from domestic circulation and even have legal sanction to ensure their media blackout. Whereas others, such as those produced by Bridle, in which the State relies upon an image-vacuum to carry out its activities with relative impunity, are surely needed.

In 2013, *Forensic Architecture*, a European Research Council project led by Principal Investigator Eyal Weizman, that I was affiliated with as Senior Research Fellow, travelled to Düsseldorf, Germany to interview a female survivor of a U.S. drone strike that had taken place in Mir Ali, Pakistan on October 4th 2010.[3] The strike killed five people including her brother-in-law. Over the course of a day, working with her lawyer and a computer modeller, the witness guided the digital reconstruction of her destroyed home locating all its architectural features and positioning personal objects within it, including her child's toys and walker. The resulting 3D model and animation was entered into the UN Drone Strike Investigation conducted by Ben Emmerson (UN Special Rapporteur for Counter Terrorism and Human Rights) in 2013 as a form of spatial evidence and presented at the UN in both New York and Geneva. This architectural visualization was essential in helping the witness recall the sequence of events of that harrowing day.

As is the case with the three sites represented in Bridle's project *Seamless Transitions*, recording devices of any kind are prohibited in the Taliban controlled tribal areas of Pakistan and therefore knowledge of drone strikes is driven by casualty statistics (numbers killed and injured). Aside from witness testimony, few visuals exist that can provide the public with information as to the extent of damage of such lethal events, the majority of which are still directed towards the domestic living spaces of local inhabitants.[4]

Our UN investigation worked from the premise that the only advantage that human rights workers had in this landscape of asymmetrical warfare was access to witnesses with whom we could work to re-create on-the-ground visualisations of drone strikes and their aftermath. And in the process also help to redress the inequity between who had the privilege of "seeing" into the space of violence and who did not. The optical sensors that permit classified visual access is available to the U.S. drone operator working at a distance thousands of kilometers away, whereas local villagers and survivors who experience a strike have only their traumatic memories and physical scars to help them remember. This image-deficit contributes to a general lack of public awareness and even arguably interest in events that seem at times far away. This is also the same visual condition that motivates much of Bridle's artwork. With few images, save the screen space of the drone operator's remote-controlled console to picture the spaces and consequences of drone warfare, the ferocious violence as well as psychological harm of this military strategy upon civilian life still largely goes unchecked.[5]

The gallery is busy today and the noisy soundscape produced by its many visitors bleeds into the viewing experience of *Seamless Transitions*, which is itself deliberately devoid of any audio that might help us understand the full register of what goes on in these digitally conjured spaces. As the acoustics of commonplace events attach themselves to the unfolding image-sequences they amplify the degree to which the dubious operations that will take place within them are also being undertaken in direct proximity to the activities of everyday life. The footsteps and conversations of the gallery visitors provide a lively syncopated soundtrack to the mute pixels of computational space. The provocation of James Bridle's project is ultimately a demand to bring these two incommensurate realms of experience together in order to produce a transformative politics: the space of public life and discourse here in the UK, and the infrastructures of violence in which logistics, architecture, State power, and the law collude to produce the smooth spaces of terror.

Further Reading: Bridle, James. *What They Don't Want You to See: The Hidden World of Uk Deportation*. The Guardian, 2015. Schuppli, Susan. *Uneasy Listening. In Forensis: The Architecture of Public Truth*, edited by Eyal Weizman, Susan Schuppli and Shela Sheikh. 381-92. Berlin: Sternberg, 2014. Tumber, Howard, and Jerry Palmer. *Media at War: The Iraq Crisis*. London: Sage, 2004.

Notes:

1. See for example his discussion of the failed deportation of Nigerian Isa Muaza. James Bridle, What They Don't Want You to See: The Hidden World of UK Deportation, The Guardian 2015.

2. See Howard Tumber and Jerry Palmer, Media at War: The Iraq Crisis (London: Sage, 2004). P. 71.

3. Forensic Architecture, Drone Strikes – Investigating covert operations through spatial media (last access: 22.02.2017).

4. See Alice Ross and Jack Serle, Most US drone strikes in Pakistan attack houses, The Bureau of Investigative Journalism, May 23 2014.

5. See for example my research into the manner in which the sound of drone surveillance is creating conditions of fear and anxiety (arguably a form of collective punishment) for those living in FATA such that the social life of communities is being irrevocably damaged. Susan Schuppli, Uneasy Listening, in Forensis: The Architecture of Public Truth, ed. Eyal Weizman, Susan Schuppli, and Shela Sheikh (Berlin: Sternberg, 2014).

James Bridle (b. 1980, UK) is a British writer, artist, publisher, and technologist. His work covers the intersection of literature, culture, and the network. Many of his works are available online. In 2011, he coined the term "New Aesthetic," and his ongoing research around this subject has been featured and discussed worldwide.

Bridle's work has been shown at the Oslo Architecture Triennale, 2016; Victoria & Albert Museum, 2015; the Southbank Centre, 2014; the Photographer's Gallery, 2012; Artangel, 2012; the 1st Istanbul Design Biennial, 2012; Guimaraes European City of Culture, 2012. As a journalist and essayist he has written for *The Guardian, The White Review, Frieze, WIRED, ICON, Domus, Cabinet, The Atlantic, The New Statesman,* and many other publications, and between 2011 and 2015 wrote a regular column for *The Observer* newspaper on publishing and technology.

Susan Schuppli (Canada/Switzerland) is an artist and researcher based in the UK, whose work examines evidence from war and conflict to environmental disasters. Through investigative processes that involve an engagement with scientific and technical modes of inquiry, her work aims to open up new conceptual pathways into the material strata of our world. She is currently Senior Lecturer and Deputy Director of the Centre for Research Architecture at Goldsmiths in London. Schuppli received her PhD from Goldsmiths and participated in the Whitney Independent Study Program after completing her MFA at the University of California San Diego. Recipient of ICP Infinity Award 2016. From 2011-14 she was Senior Research Fellow on the ERC project Forensic Architecture. Previously she was an Associate Professor in media arts in Canada.

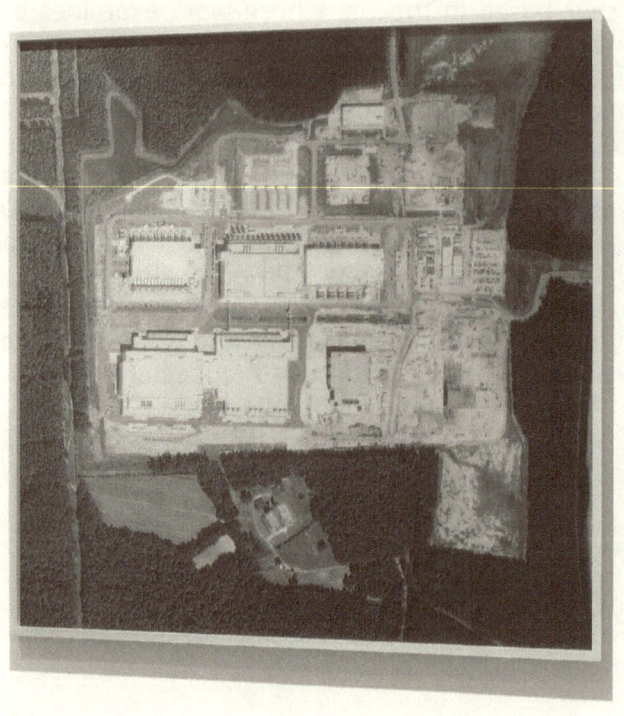

Moncks Corner, 33.064257, -80.0443453.
Ingrid Burrington

Lenticular print.
38 ½ x 39 ½ in. 100 x 100 cm.
Courtesy of the artist and NOME Gallery.

Reconnaissance

by Ingrid Burrington

Moncks Corner is part of the series *Reconnaissance*, which features satellite images of data centers, military sites, and downlinks on large-scale lenticular prints. As the viewer shifts from one side of the work to the other, the composite nature of the image is revealed: It combines two satellite photos of the site of Google's data center in Moncks Corner, South Carolina, before and after its construction, which was completed in 2007, and for which, in 2013, the corporation announced plans to build a $600-million-dollar expansion. Undertaking reciprocal evidentiary purposes, the print portrays a single, politically relevant location captured at two different points in time.

Reconnaissance juxtaposes two satellite photographs of the same location as evidence of the hidden infrastructure of power. Seeking evidence by means of aerial photography and by the forensic analysis of before-and-after images are investigative practices essential for demanding accountability from state and corporate structures. The series makes use of satellite vision to expand ways of seeing and, along with them, the reference points of political, social, and physical reality.

Crucial Nodes Designed To Be Ignored

by Aude Launay

In the future, our bilateral relations with Google will be just as important as those we have with Greece,[1] declared Anders Samuelsen, Denmark's Minister for Foreign Affairs, at the closing of the quite troubled first month of 2017.

Despite the fact that opening a text with the phrase "in the future" is funny, this statement has the quality of a truism and, above all, it hit the headlines bringing back to light the term "TechPlomacy." How strange it is that such an accurate portmanteau hasn't yet found its way as the ultimate buzzword, because that's exactly what it is about, after all. Just like oil trade used to run the debates at the core of international relationships, now that tech companies are ranking at the top of the world's most valuable companies, this oxymoron had to be unveiled. It's henceforth the dependency and reliance of states on Silicon Valley products that is at stake.

Welcoming the setting up of data centers on its territory has become for the chosen country the equivalent of the establishment of factories in the 20th century, due to the outrageous economic weight they represent in terms of power, water supply, and global physical investment on the territory, nonetheless with a way more modest workforce. And as our Danish Minister usefully reminds us, "some [of these companies] also have a size that is comparable to nations."[2] If those massive brick later steel buildings that signaled the advent of the industrial park in the suburban landscape haven't been subject to a specifically intense interest per se, data centers tend to appear shrouded in mystery, which makes them a recent topic of interest for researchers in diverse fields. While some of them are heavily branded by the companies that use them (Facebook welcomed journalists into its gigantic Swedish facility, its CEO himself posting pictures of it on his profile while Google produced a 360° video of a guided tour of its data center in Oregon), others rather resemble well-guarded secrets, sorry, buildings. We could surely say that

Ingrid Burrington started to look at them more closely as a natural continuation of the curiosity about the physicality of the Internet she's been developing in her artistic practice for already something like seven years now, and it would be fine. But the specificity of her perspective lies in the way she conducts her research: she's not a studio artist mainly looking at the Internet from the Internet, she frequently hits the road to investigate on-site the object of her interest: the Internet's infrastructure. Then she writes articles about it.

One of her primary concerns is the economic bond that ties defense and surveillance to private companies. And it's while exploring the places that embody surveillance, and in particular the NSA headquarters area, that she learnt about what was to become one of her fetish companies: Corporate Office Properties Trust, a real-estate agency specialized in offices for defense contractors and data center properties. In order to delineate the history of this increasing privatization of the military-industrial complex, Ingrid Burrington began to examine satellite imagery published by the US Geological Survey and to compare the images over time. A whole series of works, titled "Reconnaissance," emerged from that process. *Moncks Corner* is one of them. *Moncks Corner*, South Carolina houses a Google data center about which very few details have been disclosed so far: its construction was announced in 2006-07, and its extension in 2013. Although the Alphabet subsidiary now proudly displays full screen pictures of its facilities, these very vague dates are all we'll learn about its installation on the site. The *Reconnaissance* works are all made of two images, each from a different moment in time, combined in a lenticular print, square in the way Landsat views appear when they're browsed and uploaded, but also as the tiles that compose most of the web maps nowadays, seemingly ordering Earth's territory by precomputing it in parcels just as meridians and parallels were defined to rationalize it. In *Moncks Corner*, Burrington melts a view from 2006 with one from 2016. What do they show? First, a somewhat deserted rectangle in a seemingly dry area, then the same rectangle filled with a bunch of rectangle buildings surrounded by lush greenery. Nothing exciting from above, nothing much more engaging for the curious folks who would try the Google Street View option, for instance. Crucial nodes of the global network through which our communications travel every day are decidedly discreet. More so, in the artist's words, "they're designed to be ignored." Why? Not only to secure their users' emails and privacy, but mainly because communication networks "have been weaponized, militarized"[3] by governments. Which is nothing new or, at least, has an entire history leading up to this situation. Let's not forget that the highways which allowed for the setting up of these data centers[4] in suburban zones as much as the aerial imagery based on orbiting satellites and the GPS technology itself have all been originally developed for military purposes. "More than any other big tech company, Google has really normalized the satellite image vantage point to the average consumer without military clearance," adds Burrington.

The thing is, Google Earth "create[s] a composite "false" image of the distributed surface of the Earth by integrating the perspectives of multiple orbital satellite perspectives into one (interactive) visual totality."[5] Whether we agree or not on his "stack" description/metaphor, Benjamin Bratton judiciously talks about "economies of mutual stimulation between land, image, and interface by redefining the surface of the Earth as a living and governable epidermis."[6] And this mutual stimulation, euphemistic wording as for the situation Google Earth and Google Maps find themselves in, can also be described in this case as the rise of the interface sovereignty. So yes, "the continuous collection and utilization of land remote sensing data from space are of major benefit in studying and understanding human impacts on the global environment, in managing the Earth's natural resources, in carrying out national security functions, and in planning and conducting many other activities of scientific, economic, and social importance,"[7] but it also gave rise, in Google's use of this data, to a new sort of governance, overarching trans-territoriality to become, as we know, a supra-territoriality. Numerous examples[8] of which could be given, leading to critical situations in some cases, such as when after having placed an historically contested Costa Rican island on the Nicaraguan zone on Maps, Google's "image" thus produced has been used as a proof to justify an invasion of the territory by Nicaraguan forces.[9] What are Ingrid Burrington's images an evidence of? Of an indistinct moment, of a gap in time, of an invisible fact the occurrence of which we can only infer from the "resulting" image we see of it. They surely raise more questions than they provide evidence. At first sight.

It has become commonplace for the powerful (whichever power they can claim: state or financial) to ask for their erasure from these digital maps, which is quite often accepted. After all, Google is a private company and can't claim state power. It's sometimes even taken into account before the sale of the images to Google—or to any other satellite-driven mapping service provider—but the terms of these negotiations are not disclosed. Unlike traditional mapping, the satellite image is considered truer to its subject due to its partially unmanned production: the distinctiveness of the map, that is to say the fact that it represents the territory as much as it creates it, thus applies to it even more. Most of the time, the map emphasizes the state as territorial or spatial entity: it's the most traditional manifestation of state power. The legal issues that ensue the use of satellite imagery for mapping are fascinating: which should be the applicable legislation to the view of a territory: the one of the country where the satellite is registered or the one of the country that appears on the image? Google buys the rights of the majority of the images it uses. Who should be governing these images? Of course, this raises the issue of a supra authority, but isn't that strange that such a mapping service is customized according to the place where the user is based? It is now generally acknowledged that "platforms have assumed and absorbed several core political functions of the modern state"[10] and it is becoming the consensus that data is subject to the laws of the country/jurisdiction in which it is stored, but data is far from being only at rest and it's essentially in transit. This is where the sovereign power of data bunkers comes into play, and if the word bunker can at times be understood metaphorically in the sense of "fortified locations in the cloud for data storage,"[11] it has to be noted that "many highly publicized data centers [...] have located themselves in former military installations."[12]

And with this notion of bunker comes the one of encryption, which seems so far the solution to jurisdiction concerns when data traverses geographical borders. It is also interesting to notice that Google boldly communicates about its former military personnel employees, in particular in the Berkeley county where *Moncks Corner* is situated. The communication strategy used by Google concerning its data centers definitely remains unclear, and this is the main fact that Ingrid Burrington highlights in her part of the *Reconnaissance* series dedicated to the company's data centers. The traceability of their construction appears fragmented, just like the records of the satellite images' modifications. History loses its steadiness in the digital era as "parts of our intellectual record are disappearing in such a way that we cannot even tell that they have ever existed"[13] as Julian Assange once outlined while discoursing on the page not found issue, which doesn't say more than this, even when a story "was removed as the result of a legal threat," for instance.

If the demand for transparency is a subject on its own that we can't even skim here, Burrington's images seem to mirror this production of a new geography we are witnessing, a geography that reconfigures influences and networks in their inextricable entanglement with state and corporate governances, while computational governance dissolves in a "platform immanence."[14] A composite of already composite images, the images in the *Reconnaissance* series underline the difficulty that lies in trying to access two opposite ideas at the same time with the same clarity of mind, and the fact that "maps of horizontal global space can't account for all the overlapping layers that create a thickened vertical jurisdictional complexity."[15] They enable the production of a third image, an image which only lies in the eye of the viewer, possibly the image that both companies like Google and intelligence organizations like the NSA forbid to mechanically produce of their facilities.[16] Possibly also an image of the kind artificial intelligence systems developed by these same companies and agencies can now create. A physical and deliberately low tech version of a generative adversarial neural network. An image of the event that had not been recorded by the satellite, an image of the missing moment in the history record.

Notes:

1. Hilary McGann for CNNmoney: *Denmark will get world's first tech ambassador* (published on January 27th, 2017)

2. Adam Taylor for The Washington Post: *Denmark is naming an ambassador who will just deal with increasingly powerful tech companies* (Published on February 4th, 2917)

3. Ingrid Burrington, *Deep Lab Lecture Series*, Dec. 9, 2014

4. "we forget that the legislation that funded much of the U.S. highway system was called the National Interstate and Defense Highways Act of 1956." Ingrid Burrington, *Why Amazon's Data Centers Are Hidden in Spy Country*, Jan. 8, 2016, The Atlantic.

5. Benjamin Bratton, *The Stack, On Software and Sovereignty*, The MIT Press, 2015, p. 87.

6. Ibid.

7. The Land Remote Sensing Policy Act of 1992, article 1

8. Lots has been written in the press about the moving boundaries on Google Maps and the scandals they caused. But the most scandalous things surely are the way the private sector interferes in supposedly public law issues such as the outlining of state boundaries and the highly questionable solution chosen by Google that is to determine contested boundaries according to the opinion in use in the country from which they are being looked at on the Internet.

9. For more, see: *Google maps error sparks invasion of Costa Rica by Nicaragua*, The Telegraph, 2010)

10. Benjamin Bratton, op.cit., p. 119.

11. Tung-Hui Hu, *A Prehistory of the Cloud*, The MIT Press, 2016, p81.

12. Ibid., p. 91.

13. Hans Ulrich Obrist, *In Conversation with Julian Assange*, e-flux journal, *The Internet Does Not Exist*, Sternberg Press, 2015, p. 237.

14. Benjamin Bratton, op.cit., p. 112.

15. Benjamin Bratton, op.cit., p. 4.

16. Ingrid Burrington, *On the Outskirts of Crypto City: The Architecture of Surveillance*, Creative Time Reports, Jan.7, 2014.

Ingrid Burrington (b. 1987, U.S.) is an artist and researcher focusing on mapping, documenting, and identifying elements of network infrastructure, drawing attention to the often overlooked or occluded landscapes of the Internet. By examining the geographic contexts and material realities of the network, she seeks to both demystify these technologies and to articulate the underlying politics and power dynamics of networked systems and life within an increasingly networked society. Burrington is a member of Deep Lab, a collective that explores topics of control, power, and politics as they pertain to technology and society.

Ingrid Burrington was artist in residence at the Lower Manhattan Cultural Council, 2011; Eyebeam, 2014; the Center for Land Use Interpretation, 2015; and a fellow at Data & Society Research Institute, 2015 - present. She has written for *Art Quarterly*, *e-flux journal*, *Creative Time Reports*, *The Nation*, and *The Atlantic*. She is a frequent public speaker, and has given talks at FutureEverything, 2015; Eyeo, 2015; Theorizing the Web, 2016; and the Copenhagen Documentary Festival, 2016.

Aude Launay (b. 1983, France) is an independent curator and art critic. She is also the associate chief editor of 02, a French contemporary art review. She holds a MA in Philosophy from the University of Nantes. Between 2005 and 2016, she has been associate curator at Zoo galerie, a non-profit art space dedicated to emerging artists in Nantes. She is one of the founding members of the Belleville Biennale in Paris and she's been a curator there from 2010 to 2014. From 2012 to 2014, she's also been a lecturer in art theory at ESADSE (Ecole Supérieure d'Art et Design de St Etienne). As a curator, she partly focuses on abstract painting issues and has curated various shows in that context between 2009 and 2014, notably as part of the Biennale de Belleville in Paris; and at the Fondation d'entreprise Ricard in Paris, but also on ethical and philosophical concerns such as humanity and its environment, be it architectural or technological. She recently curated Welcome to Ecuador, an exhibition around the figure of Julian Assange.

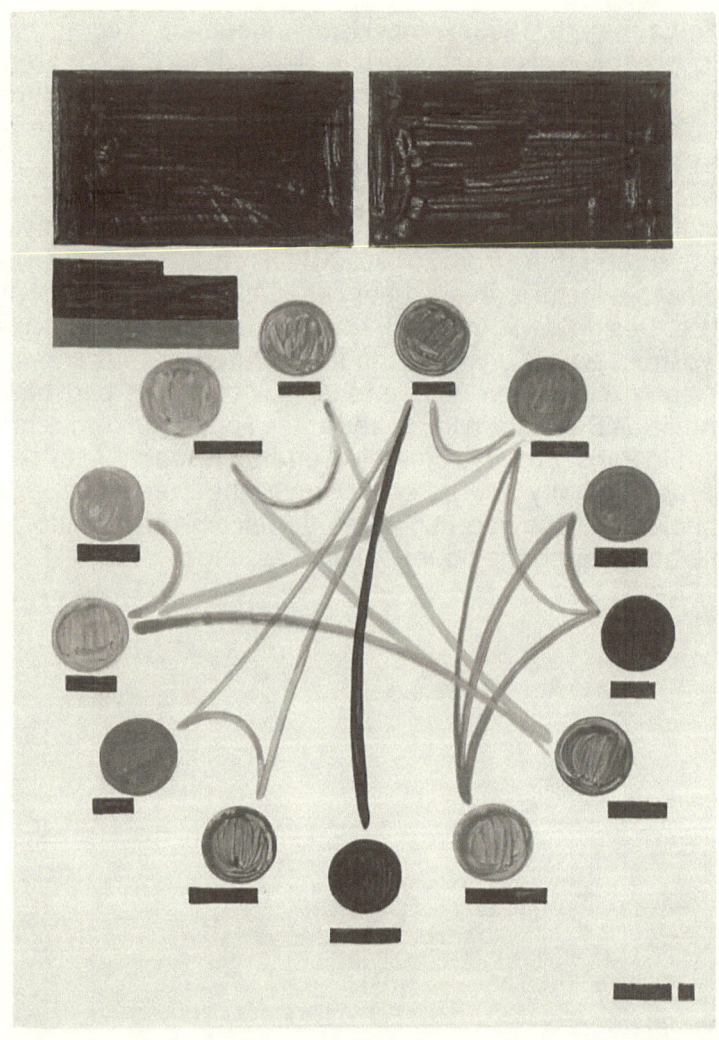

Strange Bedfellows, 2016
Navine G. Khan-Dossos

Gouache on board.
Each 10 x 14 x 1/2 in. 25 x 35 x 1,5 cm.
Courtesy of the artist and NOME Gallery.

Expanding and Remaining

by Navine G. Khan-Dossos

Expanding and Remaining is a series of panel paintings of ISIS's online English-language magazine, *Dabiq*. With the disturbing content of the publication removed, the structures of its layouts are laid bare. *Strange Bedfellows* is an infographic taken from the magazine's fifth issue, which states: "Parties that display friction or outright aggression toward one another are finding themselves aligned in a desire to counter Islamic State. Groups of coloured lines between parties represent shared interests." *If I Were The US President Today (John Cantlie) I - IV* is a four-page article written in the voice of the only British hostage still held by ISIS.

Expanding and Remaining outlines evidence of the use of modern media language as a weapon of war. The panel paintings abstractly synthesize the visual language aimed to seduce potential ISIS followers with graphic design and images. The work explores visual language as evidence and its documentary function in complex modern conflicts.

An Unfolding Interface

by Natasha Hoare

The endless cycle of idea and action,
Endless invention, endless experiment,
Brings knowledge of motion, but not of stillness;
Knowledge of speech, but not of silence;
Where is the wisdom we have lost in knowledge?
Where is the knowledge we have lost in information?

—T.S Eliot, *The Rock*, 1934.

The truth has never seemed more at stake than now as we stand at the precipice of 2017. Amidst the rapid bending of language in which "Newspeak" phrases—"fake news", "alternative facts", "incomplete facts"—worthy of George Orwell are regularly coined, the novelty of the "post-truth" moniker conceals historic precedents of manipulation of facts. Indeed, when the truth is undermined through the widespread acceptance of lies as equivalent in value to a paradigmatic shift, the proverbial canary in the coalmine, signals the rise of fascism. Within this new regime of "truth" journalism has reached a crisis point. Online news sites and social media platforms replace traditional media, driven by clickbait, beholden to no standards of conduct, distributed rapidly online to recruit fighters, shape the outcome of elections, sow scandals, misdirect, and disseminate propaganda. What does art look like in the echo chamber?

This seismic shift in world politics has been accompanied by the acceleration in the complexity of the computational systems that shape the world today. From high speed trading algorithms to cloud computing, drone warfare to mechanized agriculture, immaterial global processes, and their very real infrastructures, dictate material outcomes such as war, austerity and economic downturn. These largely lie (we are perhaps encouraged to believe) beyond the scope of human comprehension, such that some artists have responded to a call for a new imaginary to be built with which we can navigate the miasma. Art, in an evidentiary realist mode, steps in to propose new modalities for grappling with this imagistic problem. In this, they are working with, and against, similar tools to those employed by regimes and terrorist organizations who marshal the potency of memes, image, and animation to spread propaganda and destabilize world systems. Self-conscious counter-imagery and drives towards the "truth" become a pressing task taken up by some artists—provoking the coining of a new term; "evidentiary realism."

Approaching the work of Navine G. Khan-Dossos through this frame leads to a conversation regarding the nature of artistic research. An artist's methodology is not necessarily ethically anchored, and their relationship to "truth" is not defined. Dossos's research, whilst meticulous and in depth, is rooted in the potential for a translation of information to painterly form, with a particular emphasis on the materiality and dictates of paint and ground as her medium. This movement towards abstraction pushes a relationship to "evidence" or "realism", understood as providing access to a reality, but whose content enters into the spirit of the terms' claim towards the documentary in art.

Dossos's work does refer directly to current affairs, particularly the mediation of Daesh. It also has an embedded stylistic relationship to 'truth'. In earlier works, she references the forms of aniconism; an Islamic tradition of abstraction with a specific relationship to art as a pathway to truth. In the use of fractals, related to Golden Age advances in mathematics and geometric theory, artists and craftsmen employing aniconic forms in architecture, textiles, painting, and other media, mapped the divine truth of creation through an algorithmic aesthetic; Dossos draws on Laura Mark's account of aniconism in relation to new media art, Marks proposes an "aesthetics of unfolding and enfolding whereby an image acts as an interface with information, and information acts as an interface for the infinite."[1]

Dossos tools this approach to consider contemporary realities. In her work the fractal pattern becomes intimately related to the pixel, the visual unit through which our relationship to world events is mediated. In the wall painting *My TV Ain't HD, That's Too Real*, 2015 one layer of tessellated forms (a NASA image of a sun-synchronous orbit), scaled to a standard TV monitor size, uses colors drawn from Daesh's video of the execution of journalist James Foley. The same video was analyzed by British investigative Eliot Higgins, who geo-located the exact site of the execution using satellite imagery of Raqqa, Syria. Here, one story elicits two very different responses—a forensic analysis used to provide evidence of the "true" site of the killing, and an abstraction of the same information into a painterly interface whose referent unfolds over time, whose beauty wrong-foots the viewer, leading her into a contemplation of Foley's death and its world wide mediation. The two operate with vastly different strategies, but both move towards a truthful understanding of the brutality of the journalist's murder and its weaponization by Daesh on a global platform.

In her more recent work, Dossos has produced a series of panels that distill spreads of *Dabiq*, an online recruitment magazine for Daesh, into abstract forms using colors drawn from RGB and CYMK palettes; speaking to the functionality of color in digital technology and print. The works are also distributed as PDFs through the website *Ibraaz*, mimicking *Dabiq's* own distribution. Here Dossos moves away from the perhaps problematic beauty and abstraction of fully-fledged aniconism, instead reducing and isolating the graphic structural components the organization decided would appeal to its readers whilst abstracting these to cut their ongoing exchange and distribution. New works from the series *INFOESQUE* take as their source *Rumiyah*, the magazine that since 2016 has replaced *Dabiq*. *Rumiyah* breaks with *Dabiq* in moving the terrorist's aesthetic to incorporate overtly Islamic arabesque forms—drawing on an aesthetic tradition as a statement of authority. The paintings reproduce the arabesque forms and redact the accompanying texts, leaving the arches and swirls hanging in flat space, through isolation reiterating their almost surreal deployment. Strangely, after bit rot has set in, Dossos's panels may be all that is left of the original magazines—a last painterly echo. Dossos proposes a black mirror[2] to our post-truth contemporary paradigm of constant crisis, one that distills complexity to abstracted form, itching at deeper truths whilst maintaining a truth to her medium.

Notes:

1. Marks, L. Enfoldment and Infinity, An Islamic Genealogy of New Media Art. 2010, MIT Press.

2. Black Mirror here refers to the Claude Glass; a small convex dark tinted mirror used by landscape painters in the 18th and 19th century. When viewing a landscape through the glass it was usefully reduced in both form and color, lending itself to translation into a painted image.

Navine G. Khan-Dossos (b. 1982, London) is a visual artist. Her interests include Orientalism in the digital realm, geometry as information and decoration, and image calibration. Khan-Dossos uses painting to meld geometric abstraction with the traditional aniconism of Islamic art. She approaches painting— from egg tempera on wood panel to wall works and murals— as an "informational" act in which fields of knowledge are built from 'the conflicted and complex relationship of Islam to the West'.

She has exhibited and worked with institutions including Serpentine Galleries, London, 2016; the Museum of Islamic Art, Doha, 2016; the Benaki-Museum, Athens, 2016; Witte de With, Rotterdam, 2015; the Jan Van Eyck Academie, Maastricht, 2015; the Delfina Foundation, London 2015; Leighton House Museum, London, 2008; and the A.M. Qattan Foundation, Ramallah, 2007.

Natasha Hoare (b. 1984, UK) is a curator and critic. She has been Curator at Witte de With Center for Contemporary Art, Rotterdam since 2014. She holds an MA in Curating from Chelsea College of Art and Design, London, and a BA in English Literature from Edinburgh University.

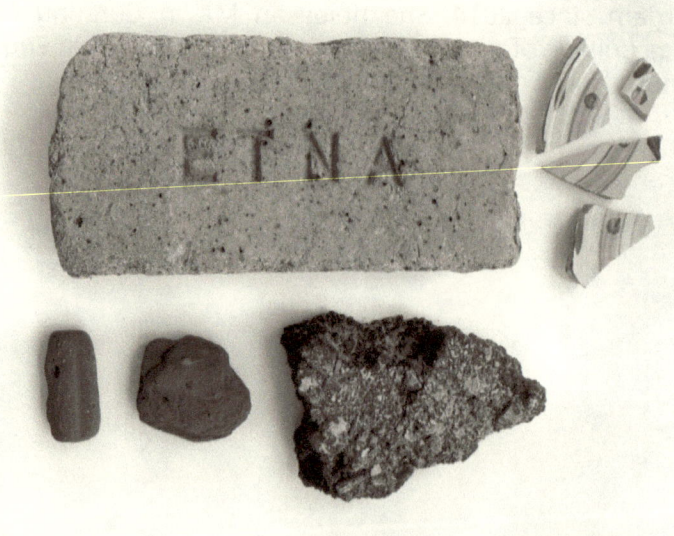

Lalla Road, Icacos, Trinidad and Tobago, 10.060458,-61.927480.
September 10, 2016
Balkin, et al.

Ceramic plate shards; glazed clay; road fragments, asphalt, stones, sand.
Courtesy of the archive (Balkin, et al.).
Alicia Milne and Luis Vasquez La Roche.
Photo: Milne/La Roche.

A People's Archive of Sinking and Melting

by Amy Balkin

A People's Archive of Sinking and Melting is a collection of objects related to the physical, political, and economic impacts of climate change. The collaborative project draws on an open call for items from around the world, composing a public record of community-gathered evidence of the effects of rising sea levels, coastal erosion, and desertification.

A People's Archive of Sinking and Melting assembles evidence of the effects of global warming and their social consequences. The ready-made sculptural works portray environmental and social impacts of climate change through a social process driven by the artist's concept, exploring the participatory aspect of evidence collecting.

An Archive of Evidence

by Blanca de la Torre

Year 2068. 44 states have disappeared, in particular the 44 countries that formed the AOSIS, a coalition created in 1990 of small islands and low-lying coastal countries vulnerable to the effects of climate change. The steps taken after each COP since the first one in Berlin and the Kyoto Protocol two years after were never fulfilled, and they wouldn't have been enough. Apart from the total disappearance of these ones, a considerable number of areas are under the threat of extinction, and have been facing a whole range of natural disasters—floods, hurricanes, tsunamis, toxic soil, polluted underground water. It started with Kiribati, the first country devastated due to global warming, where, decades ago, the government acquired 6,000 hectares of terrain in Fiji, 2,200 km south, to be able to relocate its population. After it other countries started falling like dominos. And it's not over...

This could be the stereotypical dystopic landscape from a cliché introduction to any dime science fiction book. It even sounds ridiculously reiterative to insist on the fact that this is already happening. Just as I am writing these lines, there is a huge crevice rapidly growing in the Larsen C ice shelf, in West Antarctica, that could soon be one of the ten biggest icebergs on the planet, approximately 5,000 sq. km. Larsen A and Larsen B were already lost years ago, in 1995 and 2002 respectively.

A permanent state of cynicism seems to be the pattern. Confronted with this situation, understanding scientific facts is not enough, and art presents itself as a viable tool of knowledge to contribute to the public debate, through artistic proposals that may offer alternative ways and viewpoints to the current ecocide.

For Timothy Morton environmentalist writing seems like "patching up the void with duct tape." Many solutions seem either out of date or inadequate in their attempt to generate different ways of making us feel regarding the state we are in, without changing it, and environmental art and politics are no exception. For the philosopher of the so-called Dark Ecology, Eco-critique could establish collective forms of identity that include other species and their worlds, both real and possible.[1]

For David Haley, the role of art here becomes clear: "As humankind starts to recognize that apocalyptic change is imminent, the *practice of art(s) may be an essential discipline to emerge beyond collapse* ... [t]urning the face of disaster to the face of opportunity, this paradigm shift attempts "to bring the whole to life "through" growth ecology."[2]

Amy Balkin is one of the artists whose work turns that face of disaster, combining cross-disciplinary research and social critique in her often participatory projects, which have usually been concerned with climate change and its effects.

This is the case in *A People's Archive of Sinking and Melting*, a collaborative project in the form of an ongoing archive of heterogeneous objects from places where climate change is implicated in either current or future disappearance, which Balkin has been developing since 2011.

In the beginning, Balkin had the idea of participation in mind and was inspired by the community-oriented archives of the People's Museum in Birzeit, Palestine, a museum of self-representation based on contributions collected through dialogue, and the Donora Smog Museum in Pennsylvania. The latter houses materials documenting a deadly 1948 air inversion of smog that trapped air pollution from U.S. Steel's Zinc Works and American Steel & Wire, sickening and killing residents there. It also triggered the clean-air movement through the first Air Pollution Control Act of 1955 in the United States.

As of 2017, the archive contains contributions from Anvers Island (Antarctica), Australia, Cape Verde, Santiago de Cuba, Germany, Greenland, Iceland, Venice (Italy), Kivalina (Alaska), Mexico, Nepal, New Orleans, New York, Panama, Peru, Republic of Komi (Russia), California, Senegal, and Tuvalu. The last ones, presented here, are from Trinidad and Tobago, oddly enough the earliest-settled part of the Caribbean: *Ceramic Plate Shards*, *Red Clay Brick Shards*, and *Broken Road and Dislodged Firebrick*, contributed by Alicia Milne and Luis Vasquez de La Roche.

Participation here is a keystone, as in most of Balkin's body of work, not only in the making process but as a crucial part of the discourse. In this case it has been created with all the contributors who sent the objects, along with co-registrars, including Malte Roloff and Cassie Thornton.

There are many aspects to consider regarding how history is written and rewritten: who does it, from where, and for whom. With this testimonial archive Balkin opens up different modes for this "writing" while sharing it with her collaborators. Some of these co-authors answer a survey after sending the objects, recontextualizing the double testimony: that of the experience and the objects themselves. These become another type of evidence that stress the real fact, not only the scientific records related to natural disasters (should we continue naming them "natural"? Or, is this just another way of avoiding responsibility?). This responsibility in writing history beckons us to rethink the modes of preservation of the past and its cultural representation.

In this sense the archive operates from the principle that anything is equally valuable as a record. The resulting sort-of-readymades achieve the extra value of that evidence. Regardless of whether the debris is natural or manufactured, found or discarded as trash. There are no scales of value, all forming part of a chronicle of loss.

Therefore, knowledge is co-created, where evidence of climate change is the epicenter of an amalgam of relationships between people and their relationship to places, revealing the economic, political, and social layers that underlie them.

When the artist is asked about this evidence, she points out the archive might serve, in exhibit and testimony, as potential "criminal" evidence,[3] not scientific evidence, as gathered from sites of "slow violence."[4]

Evidence of the "accumulation by dispossession,"[5] as David Harvey says, as the main victims of the fossil fuel economy of the so-called developed countries are especially small island nations.

An evidence that, as the title of the work suggests itself—People's Archive—ends up being collective. Could we hence speak about "collective evidence"? A collective evidence where the spectator takes part too, shared by the contributors, either the ones that live where the objects come from or the passersby. The feelings among them might be different and that's when the notion of empathy would play a crucial role. Like one of the interviewees explains: "I purchased the carved whale vertebrae from a resident of Kivalina, an artist named Russell Adams Jr. The people there are primarily Inupiat and have lived in the area thousands of years through subsistence; hunting bowhead whale is a large part of that tradition and culture. I contributed because I think climate change is the single greatest issue facing humanity right now. Already we are seeing Inuit populations losing an entire way of life, because of global warming's radical effects on the Arctic. This is the beginning, and we need to pay attention, and feel, and act, before the only option becomes reacting to the inevitable."

The work immediately functions as a kind of time-machine, bringing the public towards a possible future society that would find the archive, like an archeological discovery that opens up to those places lost due to human hubris.

We cannot be sure that all those places in danger will disappear, some may and others may not, but since the threat is there, steps are to be taken and the possibility is already present. A fear of losing a home, place, roots, heritage. The alarm of no return, no possibility of looking back.

This brings us to the figure of the "climate refugee," a category that is not yet recognized by ACNUR, even though it assisted the victims of natural catastrophes, like the Tsunami of the Indian Ocean in 2004. According to the International Organization for Migration future forecasts vary from 25 million to 1 billion environmental migrants by 2050, moving either within their countries or across borders, on a permanent or temporary basis, with 200 million being the most widely cited estimate.[6]

Razmig Keucheyan, in *Nature is a Battlefield,* points out how these refugees are sometimes presented as the "missing link" that attaches economic crisis to the political tensions that may ultimately result.[7] The status of the migrant and the refugee are quite different, and Keucheyan reminds us that migrations related to climate always existed, like the Dust Bowl recalled by John Steinbeck in *The Grapes of Wrath*, portraying the migration of the Southwest during the Great Depression, victims of the dust storms.[8]

The structure of the archive is organized based on the idea of "common but differentiated," in reference to the phrase used by the UNFCCC Annex Party "common but differentiated responsibility," in relation to the liability of countries depending on their contribution and benefits from their CO2 emissions and other greenhouse gases. This approach would reflect on the varying impact that climate politics have upon different states, communities and areas of "conflict."

The compilation operates then as an archive of evidence, not only an evidence of climate change, but of the unequal political relationships, of the ecological debt of the North with the South, of postcolonialism, environmental racism, of unfairness and imbalance. But at the same time, it speaks about solidarity, empathy, and the importance of activism and the movements of environmental justice as a common goal.

These objects are spoken of as byproducts because, as Cassie Thornton explains, "it formalizes the relationship between the objects and their common origins."[9] An archive of detritus from industrial capitalism, that opens up a path of symbolic resilience through the testimonies of the Capitalocene, as Donna Haraway proposes taking the term coined by Andreas Malm and Jason Moore, to name this era instead of the hackneyed Anthropocene.[10]

Balkin's archive, intended to support cultural equity and self-representation, works as a direct and straight good answer to T. J. Demos's question: "How can artistic practices, operating at the rocky juncture of art institutions, activism and non-governmental policies, challenge the emergence of a neo-liberal eco-governmentality? How can art oppose the commercialization of nature, packaged as an economic resource, or counteract greenwashing to alternatively define the environment with a paths to define the environment a focus on global justice and ecological sustainability?"[11]

Notes:

1. Timothy Morton, Ecology Without Nature: Rethinking Environmental Aesthetics. (Cambridge, Massachusetts and London: United Kingdom: Harvard University Press, 2007), 140-141.

2. David Haley, "Seeing the Whole: Art, Ecology and Transdisciplinarity. Arte y Políticas de identidad," Servicio de publicaciones de la universidad de Murcia, vol. 4 (2011).

3. Monica Westin, interview on Amy Balkin, Artists in Conversation BOMB July 2, 2015 (last access 20.02.2017).

4. Rob Nixon, Slow Violence and the Environmentalism of the Poor. (Cambridge, Massachusetts: Harvard University Press, 2013)..

5. David Harvey, The New Imperialism. (Oxford: Oxford University Press, 2003).

6. International Organization for Migration (IOM): Migration and Climate Change (Last access 20.02.2017).

7. Razmig Keucheyan, La naturaleza es un campo de batalla. (Madrid: Clave intelectual, 2016), 172-174

8. Op.Cit.

9. Dana Kopel, What Will Have Been: Interviews on A People's Archive of Sinking and Melting Brooklyn Rail, June 5, 2014 (last access 20.02.2017).

10. Donna J. Haraway, Staying with the Trouble: Making Kin in the Chtulucene (Durham: Duke University Press, 2016), 101.

11. T.J. Demos, Decolonizing Nature: Contemporary Art and the Politics of Ecology (Berlin: Sternberg Press, 2016), 54.

Amy Balkin (b. 1967, U.S.) is an American artist whose work combines cross-disciplinary research and social critique to generate ambitious, bold, and innovative ways of conceiving the public domain outside current legal and discursive systems. Her projects propose a reconstituted commons, considering legal borders and systems, environmental justice, and equitable sharing of common-pool resources in the context of climate change.

Her work and documentation has been included in *Rights of Nature* at Nottingham Contemporary, 2015; at Kunsthal Aarhus, 2015; Les Abattoirs, Toulouse, 2015; dOCUMENTA 13, 2012; Mills College Art Museum, 2015; Centre Pompidou-Metz, 2016. Recent publications include *Decolonizing Nature*, 2016; *Art in the Anthropocene*, 2015; *Materiality*, 2015; *Critical Landscapes: Art, Space, Politics*, 2015. Amy Balkin studied at Stanford University and is based in San Francisco.

Blanca de la Torre (b. 1977, Spain) is an independent curator and art critic. She has curated exhibitions internationally in places such as New York, Prague, London and Madrid. From 2009 to 2013, she acted as Chief Curator at Artium, Basque Museum-Center of Contemporary Art of Vitoria-Gasteiz, Spain.

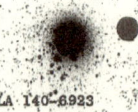

LA 140-6923

RESULTS OF INVESTIGATION

Employment

United States Post Office
300 North Los Angeles Street
Los Angeles, California

On March 14, 1969, LOUIS SMITH, Personnel Office,
advised that RODNEY ELLIS BARNETTE is still employed as a
substitute carrier at the Del Valle Station, 1237 South
Flower Street, Los Angeles, California.

Miscellaneous

On February 24, 1969, SAs JAMES W. MC CORD and
THEODORE M. GARDNER attempted to interview RODNEY ELLIS
BARNETTE. BARNETTE advised the Agents that he had nothing
to say to them.

The employee's brother AUBREY BARNETTE, was
investigated under the Federal Employees' Security Program
in 1961 and 1963. Reports were furnished to the Civil
Service Commission on October 17, 1961, and June 7, 1963,
entitled "AUBREY BARNETTE, Post Office Department, Security
of Government Employees." The Civil Service Commission advised
on January 19, 1962, that a "favorable determination" was
reached in BARNETTE'S case. A supplemental investigation was
conducted on BARNETTE in 1967 when he was employed by the Small
Business Administration and reports were furnished to the Civil
Service Commission on June 13, 1967.

My Father's FBI File: Government Employees, 2017
Sadie Barnette

Archival pigment prints, 22 × 17 in. 55,8 × 43,1 cm. each, edition of 5
Courtesy of the artist and Charlie James Gallery.

My Father's FBI File

by Sadie Barnette

My Father's FBI File, Project 4 comprises political and personal documents concerning the surveillance and life of Rodney Barnette, founder of the Compton, California chapter of the Black Panther Party for Self-Defense, known as Section 9-A. The artist obtained over five hundred documents about the surveillance of her father by filing a Freedom of Information Act (FOIA) on the FBI's Counterintelligence Program (COINTELPRO), which was designed to suppress the Black Panther Party during the sixties and seventies. The FBI special agents (SAs) documented decades of Rodney Barnette's daily life. Barnette's file includes cases such as his role in the Angela Davis Defense Committee, his name in the ADEX list for detention without due process, and interrogations of acquaintances and informants. Specifically, *Government Employees* reports the investigation into terminating his position with the United States Post Office by accusing him of living with a woman outside of marriage, which was deemed behavior unbecoming a government employee. Some documents contain the signature of FBI director and architect of the surveillance program, J. Edgar Hoover, who declared in 1969 that "the Black Panther Party represents the greatest threat to internal security of the country." The Racial Intelligence Section was a unit within the Intelligence Division of the FBI, established in September 1967.

In *My Father's FBI File*, the evidence collected to construct false narratives of political conflict are deconstructed in the social sphere and then reconstructed within the intimacy of personal memory. The redacted historical documents of secret programs are used as raw material and combined with documents of family history. Disaffected governmental surveillance and overreach is reclaimed through the resilient aesthetics of graffiti and portrayals of personal affections.

Ephemeral Evidence

by Sampada Aranke

There's much talk about what data *reveals* in our contemporary informational landscape: the who, what, where, and how of governmental surveillance projects. But what of the networks of purposely concealed interpersonal arrangements that produce such data? Photocopied and filed documents produce the hard evidence in Sadie Barnette's *My Father's FBI Files* (2016), a series that repurposes records from her father Rodney's time as a leader of the Black Panther Party for Self Defense (BPP). But what these documents reveal is not only an overwhelming amount of information about Rodney's day to day life, but almost more importantly, they call our attention to the relational and intimate qualities of state surveillance.

Barnette's work asks us to think about the overwhelming interpersonal contact necessitated by the FBI's Counterintelligence Program (COINTELPRO), a comprehensive intelligence gathering operation that took place between 1956 and 1971 under the leadership of FBI director J. Edgar Hoover.[1] In September 1968, just less than two years after the organization's founding, Hoover had designated the Black Panther Party for Self-Defense (BPP) as "the most dangerous threat to the internal security of the country."[2] The FBI classified the BPP's activities under the categorical designation "Black Extremist."[3] This program had successfully waged a complex network of operations aimed to discredit, dismantle, and destroy Black radical activists and organizations.[4] COINTELPRO effectively destroyed radical social movements by engaging a series of tactics, including infiltration, sabotage, arrest, false imprisonment, and, in some cases, murder.[5] The impacts of this program are lasting, from radicals who are still imprisoned based on COINTELPRO operations, to the many communities who were psychologically traumatized due to infiltration and police terror. In addition to these immediate and very material impacts, COINTELPRO advanced and expanded state intelligence programs, and indeed legitimated the surveillance, policing, and criminalization of political activists, thus justifying the suspension of legal protections and expansion of governmental power. Part and parcel of this program was the production of a jaw-dropping amount of documentation of these operations, often organized around individual political activists in an attempt to discredit and criminalize their political work, as was the case with Rodney Ellis Barnette, notable BPP organizer and founder of the Compton California chapter of the Party.

After filing for a Freedom of Information Act (FOIA) request to unseal Rodney's FBI file, Sadie and Rodney Barnette received an overwhelming amount of paperwork. Over 500 pages of FBI documents on Rodney Ellis Barnette reveal that he was followed by FBI special agents (SAs) for years, his everyday movements and activities under constant surveillance.[6] The FBI's monitoring of his everyday activities was comprehensive to say the least. It included a steady team of special agents who conducted routine surveillance, harassed people close to Barnette, and attempted to frame him with charges of illegal activities by soliciting informants to infiltrate the BPP.[7] While this governmental conspiracy thankfully never resulted in legal charges, the files expose a set of bureaucratic imperatives that aim to produce and organize the document as evidence. However, these documents evince the state's entangled and elaborate policing endeavors, all of which required a set of social relations, subjective observations, and affective binds that trouble these materials and their afterlives.

For *My Father's FBI File* (2016), Sadie re-presents 180 pages of her father's file. Rather than display these documents in their fully redacted format as she received them, Barnette has added flourishes like bright pink and purple hues or thick coats of black spray paint or glitter star stickers—sometimes she uses all off the above—to highlight moments of redaction or to reclaim phrases intended to be pejorative in reference to Rodney's activities.

In response to the racialized project of the surveillance of Black people, the series *My Father's FBI Files* mobilizes a radical Black aesthetic practice of touch and adornment as activations of Black intimacy, family, and sociality.[8] It is just as crucial to note that Sadie's project also points us to the underbelly of the evidentiary impulse within these bureaucratic documents. These papers—their consistent redactions, selective details, noted research, and banal descriptions—also point us to the *limits* of what they can conceal. Sadie amplifies the government's censorship within these documents by applying spray directly in relation to each document's inked redacted areas, thus calling our attention to our inability to access the information in its entirety. As Sadie's own compositional obfuscation highlights, some documents are almost entirely redacted while others are only composed of a handful of sentences. While some documents tell us that Rodney was seen boarding a plane with Angela Davis, others are so heavily redacted that all we are left with are a series of grammatical articles and prepositions. In our search for answers we're left with more questions.

These questions are potentially unwieldy, because if answered fully, the networks of social relations that helped to compose these documents begins to include networks of strangers, friends, and infiltrators that Rodney himself might have known. For every document, Sadie suggests, we have SAs engaging in dozens of interpersonal interactions. We are asked to consider a series of *hows*: how SAs received their information, how they coerced everyday people into being informants, how they gained access to areas without blowing their covers, how many people they spoke to, places they visited, how many days and nights they were on duty, how many phone calls they made, how many targets they followed. This is the data that has no documentary accompaniment. This data is overwhelmingly complex and traffics in the affective: intimidation, threats, charm, politeness, emotional gaslighting, blackmailing. These are the registers that are not translated onto the page.

The document, in other words, is produced and circulated by a set of ephemeral evidence— materials that cannot be captured on paper, photocopied and faxed into file cabinets around the country. This evidence exists in the realm of the relational and affective and both compose and exceed the document. Sadie's work, in its stunning display of the interpersonal as political, opens up the document as a partial frame through which we might access the ephemeral and affective contours of surveillance and policing.[9]

Notes:

1 FBI official website: https://vault.fbi.gov/cointel-pro

2 Ward Churchill and James Vanderwall, *Agents of Repression: The FBI's Secret Wars against the Black Panther Party and the American Indian Movement*, (Boston: Southend Press, 2008); Gabriel San Roman, "1969: The Year the Black Panther Party Was to Be Annihilated," *Truthout*, January 28, 2014, accessed February 27, 2017, http://www.truth-out.org/news/item/21382-1969-the-year-the-black-panther-party-was-to-be-annihilated.

3 The FBI's website preserves the original organizational logic with categories listed as: "White Hate Groups, New Left, Puerto Rican Groups, Black Extremist, Hoodwink, Cuba, Socialist Workers Party, Espionage Programs." "Black Extremist" to describe groups like the BPP is particularly relevant when we think of the FBI's recent memo regarding "Black Identity Extremists." For more see: https://assets.documentcloud.org/documents/4067711/BIE-Redacted.pdf

4 For more, see: Jim Vander Wall and Ward Churchill, *Agents of Repression*, (Cambridge: South End Press, 2002); Andres Alegria, Prentis Hemphill, Anita Johnson and Claude Marks, 2012, "COINTELPRO 101," DVD, San Francisco: Freedom Archives; Howard Alk and Mike Gray, 1971, "The Murder of Fred Hampton," DVD, Chicago: Facets Video.

5 Ibid.

6 Maria L La Ganga, "Black Panthers 50 years on: art show reclaims movement by telling 'real story.' *The Guardian*, October 8, 2016.

7 Rodney and Sadie Barnette, "A Panther's Story Becomes Art: A conversation between artist Sadie Barnette and her father and former Black Panther Rodney Barnette," *Oakland Museum of California blog*, November 4, 2016, http://museumca.org/blog/panthers-story-becomes-art

8 Sampada Aranke, "Material Matters: Black Radical Aesthetics and the Limits of Visibility," *e-flux* journal #7

9, February 2017; Sampada Aranke, "Whose 1968?: Bringing History Home in Sadie Barnette's *Dear 1968*," exhibition essay, UC Davis Art Museum, April 14-June 30, 2017.

Sadie Barnette (b. 1984, U.S.) is a California artist who investigates the unexpected locations of identity construction, family histories, subcultural coding, celebration, and excess. Barnette creates photographs, detailed drawings, and large scale installations, engaging in minimalism, text, found objects, and the personal as political for poetry and abstraction in urban life.

Barnette's work has been exhibited throughout the United States and internationally at venues including The Studio Museum, Harlem (where she was Artist in Residence, 2014-2015); the Oakland Museum of California, 2016; The Mistake Room, 2015, and Charlie James Gallery, Los Angeles, 2016; and Goodman Gallery, Johannesburg, 2015. Barnette is the recipient of *Art Matters* and *Artadia* awards, 2017, and has work featured in the permanent collections of museums such as The Pérez Art Museum, Miami; the California African American Museum, Los Angeles; and The Studio Museum, Harlem. She lives and works in California and is represented by Charlie James Gallery, Los Angeles. Barnette earned her BFA from CalArts and her MFA from the University of California, San Diego.

Sampada Aranke (b.1986, U.S.) is an Assistant Professor in the Art History, Theory, Criticism Department. Her research interests include performance theories of embodiment, visual culture, and black cultural and aesthetic theory.

CREDITS

Curated and organized by Paolo Cirio.

Produced by NOME, Berlin.
Presented in NYC with Fridman Gallery.

With the collaboration of Paula Cooper Gallery, NYC; Fridman Gallery, NYC; Pierogi Gallery, NYC; and P.P.O.W., NYC; Robert Koch Gallery, San Francisco; Charlie James Gallery, Los Angeles; Annely Juda Fine Art, London; Sprüth Magers Gallery, Berlin.

Research and assistance: Jesi Khadivi, Abraham Adams, Anna Gien, Rosario Güiraldes.

Catalogue
Editor: Paolo Cirio.
Editing: Jesi Khadivi.
Creative direction: 515 Creative Shop.
Graphic design: Zarah Landes.

NOME
Director: Luca Barbeni.
Managing Director: Olga Boiocchi.
Press: Tabea Hamperl.

Thanks to Torsten Oetken, Nino Caltabiano, Milena Maffei.

ISBN 978-0-359-46095-3